A Barista in Santa Fe
What a Long Strange Trip It's Bean

A Memoir

A BARISTA IN SANTA FE
What a Long Strange Trip It's Bean

A MEMOIR

BILL DEUTSCH

SUNSTONE
PRESS

SANTA FE

Note: The contents of this book, including any factual data, depictions, opinions, reports, dates, and characterizations are solely those of the author and Sunstone Press is not responsible nor does it take responsibility for the material or the accuracy of material presented in the content of this book.

Sunstone books may be purchased for educational, business, or sales promotional use. For information please write: Special Markets Department, Sunstone Press, P.O. Box 2321, Santa Fe, New Mexico 87504-2321.
Printed on acid-free paper

Library of Congress Cataloging-in-Publication Data

Names: Deutsch, Bill, 1953- author.
Title: A barista in Santa Fe : what a long strange trip it's bean : a memoir / Bill Deutsch.
Other titles: Barista in Santa Fe : what a long strange trip it's been
Description: Santa Fe : Sunstone Press, [2023] | Summary: "A memoir of a barista in Santa Fe, New Mexico that recounts thirty years, a million drinks, and a whole lot of customers along the way"-- Provided by publisher.
Identifiers: LCCN 2023057049 | ISBN 9781632936271 (paperback) | ISBN 9781611397307 (epub)
Subjects: LCSH: Deutsch, Bill, 1953- | Baristas--New Mexico--Santa Fe--Biography. | Santa Fe (N.M.)--Biography. | LCGFT: Biographies.
Classification: LCC F804.S253 .D48 2023 | DDC 978.956053092 [B]--dc23/eng/20240103
LC record available at https://lccn.loc.gov/2023057049

WWW.SUNSTONEPRESS.COM
SUNSTONE PRESS / POST OFFICE BOX 2321 / SANTA FE, NM 87504-2321 /USA
(505) 988-4418

Dedicated to you, my reader

PROLOGUE

This is a book about me and a lot of my customers. What I went through for thirty years, my accomplishments and my failures. This book is easy to read and even contains a miracle, as well as a secret. Well sorta, as you will come to find out. I honestly don't think any barista went through what I went through, especially to become number one. I name some names and throw in a little bit of trivia about Santa Fe, the oldest capital city in America. You will enjoy this book and find it amusing and intriguing. I believe everything is pretty much accurate. So sit back and enjoy thirty years worth of making coffee, mostly in Santa Fe.

It was like this: I was sitting in an Adirondack chair at a retreat house on Whidbey Island, Washington. It was a weekend and I was pondering my future at The Boeing Company in Seattle. That's just it: I didn't have a future. And not only that, but nobody liked Mondays, my favorite day of the workweek and I didn't feel like working around people who complained every Monday morning. This was in September of 1991. At the time, there were over four hundred espresso carts in King County and coffee was king.

So I'm thinking, while sitting in that Adirondack chair and not seeing any future at The Boeing Company, I want to become a barista. That's it! That's what I'll do for the rest of my working life: become a professional barista.

I'll own my own espresso cart and make a living by serving people caffeine. After all, I'm good with people. Proved that by working at a Subway shop in Des Moines (a Seattle suburb) a few summers earlier recouping some money I made in a bad investment: a 1975 MG Midget. That car was a trouble maker and I had to stand in front of a judge and flash my California smile to get the ticket dismissed. Anyway, I sold the Midget. Back to Subway: It was cool meeting lots of different people. Up to now, my circle of friends consisted of church and Boeing. Same-o, same-o, and meeting different people from different places now was exciting. That experience left its mark on me.

Back to the future: this is what I did after deciding to become a barista. Every day after work I would go out and research everything necessary to start an espresso business: cart, espresso machine, grinders (one regular, one de-caff,) cash register, condiment, syrups, utensils: about 66 items in all. Right down to the smallest detail (scotch tape , sticky notes, etc.) We would name the business Bill's Espresso because, well, I'm Bill.

Caffe' Darte', a local Seattle roaster, offered classes on espresso every Wednesday evening. I attended as many as I could and gathered as much information as I could. This was good. Learning a whole new trade. Not only learning how to make espresso, but putting everything together. I even found out who made neon signs because I wanted a neon sign. I would sell Caffe' D'Arte as my coffee and I have stayed with them all thirty years. I won't drink anything else.

It was fun putting everything together. I found a cart company in Seattle who already had a cart built which I agreed to buy, Easy breezy. I went around the Seattle area visiting lots of espresso carts, observing the barista and noting his or her setup. Took lots of notes. Calculated all the costs. Did my homework. Put it all together. Had to borrow from my brother Bob to fund my crazy endeavor.

Then, in the spring of 1992, sitting on the bed for two hours with Helen (that's my wife), we had to make a decision as to where to set up shop. Did we want to stay in Seattle, where it rains a lot, or did we want to move somewhere else?

We decided to move somewhere else. But where? We tried a mall in Scottsdale, Arizona because Helen's family lives in Phoenix, but that didn't work out. Then we tried The Grand Canyon, but Fred Harvey has that gig. We could have chosen a lot of places in America.

Then, out of the blue, for some strange reason, still don't know why, I suggested Santa Fe, New Mexico. What? Santa Fe? Ever been there? Nope. Know what it's like? Nope. Why do I want to go there? I don't know. Let's do it! But first, let's find out a little about it. So we subscribed to The Santa Fe New Mexican, Santa Fe's local newspaper, for a month. Santa Fe had all the usual suspects: gangs, culture, tourism, restaurants, but no espresso. We could get in on the ground floor and claim bragging rights.

So Helen and I took our two week vacation from Boeing in May and drove on down to Santa Fe to try and secure a spot for our espresso cart. We walked around town to find the perfect spot. How about here, how about there. Well, I'm here to tell you, Santa Fe didn't seem to take kindly to outsiders, especially Anglos. (My impression.) When we found a good location down on Washington Street, we walked over to City Hall to obtain the necessary permit. Well, they gave us false information, I think just to prevent us from opening an espresso cart in their town. What to do. We drove over to Villa Linda Mall (now Santa Fe Place), six miles down the road, to see if we could open our espresso cart in their mall. As luck would have it, a young woman had a cart in the mall earlier that year but only lasted a few months, thereby leaving a void.

I hate malls, at least when it comes to selling espresso, because I would have to be open seven days a week. But what could we do? We didn't want to return to Seattle empty-handed, so we signed a lease with the mall. It was better than nothing. And after all, the mall did give us prime real estate, a spot right in the middle of the mall where everybody could see us.

So we drive back to Seattle, gave Boeing our notices, reserved a U-Haul, and began packing. We're moving to New Mexico. Y'know, we could have chosen lots of other places:

eastern Washington, maybe California, how about Illinois (my home state), or even Florida where my parents lived. But no. For some crazy reason, we chose Santa Fe.

So Helen and I quit our stable jobs at The Boeing Company and ventured off into the unknown. This is crazy! I'm 38 years old and Helen is 36. Who in their right mind would leave job security and venture off into the unknown? Will we succeed? Don't know. Damn the torpedoes, full steam ahead! Hard times ahead, tho.

Didn't take long for trouble to begin. Sure, I got some friends to help me load the U-Haul, but I chose the wrong size. Too small! Had to make a phone call, drove the truck back to U-Haul, swapped out the truck, finished loading, all done. Extra work, but we got everything packed, sent my friends home and slept well that night. Our car, a Geo Metro, was hooked up to the back of the U-Haul.

Fortunately, the drive down to Santa Fe was uneventful. In other words, nothing went wrong. But I remember how scared I was driving into Santa Fe on I-25. What have I gotten myself into. Why did I leave the security of Boeing and venture off into the unknown. No healthcare, no place to live, no friends. Definitely not for the faint of heart. We dropped the espresso cart off at the mall and Tom, the mall manager, got some mall employees to help us unload. As mentioned, we were lucky to be placed right in the center of the mall and we fit right in. The mall electrician hooked us up with power and we were good to go. We ended up staying at the Warren Inn for several weeks until we could find a place to live. Meanwhile, we needed supplies, which we bought at this local restaurant supply store. Don't know what I would have done without them. Cups, lids, the usual coffee cart stuff. Sleeves hadn't been invented yet and wooden stir sticks really weren't around. The Internet as we know it wasn't around either. Our hotel room was filled with boxes. Nothing came easy.

For instance, a big mistake I made was not setting up the cart in Seattle so I would know if everything worked well together. Everything did not work well together. At the mall, the machine and the cart were not talking to each other. The cart had plumbing problems. This meant getting to know Big Jo's Hardware, very helpful, to resolve my plumbing issues. Then the espresso machine was giving me problems. I knew of no espresso machine mechanics, which meant sending it back to Seattle and getting a replacement in the interim. I suppose driving to the Albuquerque airport and picking up the replacement at a special airport location was cool. At this time I was working with a different machine which was in terrible working condition. I eventually got my original machine back. This meant taking the lousy replacement espresso machine back to the airport in Albuquerque and picking up my original machine. That old saying, if anything can go wrong it will go wrong, sure held up with me.

Our espresso cart had a fizzy maker for making Italian sodas but that wasn't working too good so I had to ask a couple of guys at the local Coca Cola distribution plant to help me out. Nice guys. Can't remember their names but they came over to the mall and gave me a real fizzy maker. Now I could make really good Italian sodas.

At last, things were going well. Only problem was, when working at a mall, I had to be open seven days a week, ten in the morning to nine in the evening. No time off except Easter and Christmas. Soon I became disillusioned. I was trapped in a mall, seven days a week, while everyone I served was out having fun. Not knowing anyone to help us out we had to do everything ourselves. But I will tell you, our busiest days, by far, were the day before Christmas and the day after Christmas. Halloween was cool with all the kids in costume.

To get all the supply boxes out of our hotel room at Warren Inn, we rented out a local storage space. This was fine until winter arrived and I'm freezing my butt off getting my supplies. I later learned it was one of the coldest winters on record. Just my luck.

After about three weeks at the Warren Inn and arguing with the manager about paying in advance, we found a government subsidized apartment complex less than a mile away. Finally, a low rent place to live.

Back at the mall. One day I made the mistake of putting some of my coffee grounds into the mall plants, y'know, as fertilizer. Big mistake, I guess. Four mall employees took it upon themselves to rebuke me. After all, I'm the outsider they could pick on.

One interesting character was a Native American. He was an alcoholic who slept outside at night. In the mall, he was a broom pusher. Always smelled liquor on his breath. Ten years later when I was at the Eldorado Hotel, he showed up at my cart. Still smelled liquor on his breath.

Starting to get burned out from working so much at the mall, we hired a young lady to work for us. At last, Helen and I could get away, if only for a few hours. Freedom! We drove up to Ski Santa Fe to hike the trails, just to get away. But we had to get back in time to close up and do the dishes.

It was around Thanksgiving 1992 that Bill Fishbein came to the cart one night. Bill is the Executive Director of The Coffee Trust, which is an organization that provides micro loans to women in Central America to diversify their income. This was the beginning of an excellent relationship that has lasted to this day. Helen and I once catered his son's Bar Mitzvah at La Fonda Hotel.

Did I tell you? My health inspector was a Russian guy who was born in Moscow and emigrated to America at the age of six. Me, being full German, had a good relationship with him. You would have liked him. It was his responsibility to inspect all the restaurants in Santa Fe. He held everyone responsible, even going so far as to have his health reports printed up in the local newspaper. He would later play an important part in our lives when we bought some property. More on that later.

I bought some table and chairs and had them placed not far from the cart in the middle of the mall. Nice. Only problem was, the tables were wobbly and drinks were being spilled, which I had to replace. Not to mention having to constantly call maintenance and have the spills cleaned up.

Gangs would skip school and come to the mall. Not

exactly good news for me. They would walk by and spit on my cart. Even had wet socks thrown at me. Eventually I hired an employee, but he stole from me. Had to call the police but the deed was done. I did get around to firing him but he took his friend, who worked for me, with him. Now I'm back to working the cart myself, but at least I don't have an employee stealing from me. A few months later I hired a woman who wanted to be paid under the table. She really couldn't make espresso but she worked nights which gave me some time off. I just had to return at nine o'clock to close up. Why did I feel I was being taken advantage of? Being the type of guy who doesn't give up, I didn't give up.

Soon, a young woman showed up who turned out to be an incredible employee. She saved the day. Knew how to make espresso. We had a good relationship. She was an affectionate person and yes, we kissed. She has since moved out of state but I don't know where.

Back in May when Helen and I were scouting out for a place to put our cart, one place was the Eldorado Hotel. We were turned down. Oh well. Then one night at the mall, November 1992, a man shows up and asked me if I was Bill Deutsch. Having said yes (that's not exactly what I said, but anyway...) he asked me if I would be interested in (having changed his mind) setting up an espresso cart at his hotel, the Eldorado Hotel. I said yes, setting in motion my future destiny. Perhaps I should say, this was the general manager of the hotel. I applied for a loan at a local bank and they agreed to loan me the money I needed to buy another espresso cart.

The next day the manager showed me where my cart would be. Inside during the winter next to the gift shop and outside under the portal during the summer. I agreed, we shook hands, and now I had my homework: getting another espresso cart and everything else that goes with it. I had the company who made my first cart now make my second cart. A nice fellow from Yellow Freight delivered the cart to the loading dock and hotel employees placed the cart to its rightful location. The Eldorado Hotel hooked me up for power. Sounds, good, right? The worst was yet come.

I had a soft opening on May 15, 1993, and started paying rent on June 1st. Now I had two espresso carts to operate. Employee hours had to be figured out. Helen and I only had one car. Not only that, but after sixteen years of marriage, Helen is now pregnant. How interesting.

While living in Seattle and working for the Boeing Company, under the best of conditions, Helen could not get pregnant. Had the usual tests done, we were good to go, but no kid.

Oh, the pressure of handling two espresso carts in a strange town. I was working a hundred hours a week. I worked the bus schedule to reach the storage facility where my supplies were just in time before it closed, but it doesn't help when the bus driver decides to stop off at the convenience store to buy something. By the time I get off the bus, it's too late, thanks to the bus driver, storage is now closed. I can't get to my supplies.

I remember one night coming home from work at the mall when Helen started going into labor pains. I put the pedal to the metal and got pulled over by the police. I got out of the car to explain to the nice policeman that I was speeding because Helen was going into labor. He told me to get back into the car and I started yelling at him. He let me go but that experience made a lasting impression on me. Just like the time a year earlier when I got pulled over for speeding on Cerrillos Road. Had to stand in front of the judge who let me go if I attended a class. Learned more about Santa Fe in that class than I could have gotten anywhere else. The policeman who taught the class told us how he had to scrape his dad off the payment after a fatal accident. My experience with Santa Fe's court system didn't end there. I can't remember how many times I've had to stand in front of the judge, but more on that later.

Our son Boaz was born in 1993. I was there in the birthing room. As soon as the doctor received Boaz out of Helen, she passed him off to me. Here I was, holding our son just a minute after he was born, in my hands. Boaz did not want to be outside of Helen's womb and looked like Edward G. Robinson fighting to get back in.

At the time, we were working the two carts. I hired another employee who knew my other employee. She was such a blessing. She plays an important part later on. So the four of us were running the two carts.

Then a young lady shows up one day and asked if she could work for me. She was really nice and I liked her so I hired her. We would have wild times together drinking rum and Coke. And yes, we kissed. Spots of Coke were still on the inside roof of the Acura when we sold it. She now lives in another town but we keep in touch.

I was working less hours now but a lesser man would have given up. I would carry our newborn son Boaz in his baby pack while I made espresso. Whatever it took to keep the business running. So I'm now running two espresso carts and wearing a kid in his baby pack while making espresso. Down to about eighty hours a week now but it was only a matter of time before I threw in the towel. There was a young woman who worked in the gift shop at the Eldorado Hotel and I think she liked me. I once asked her to drive me home to the San Rafael apartments. We both sat in the front seat and yes, we kissed.

At this point in time, nothing much happened at the Eldorado Hotel, as far as I was concerned. The espresso carts were my business and I was too consumed to be involved in anything else. Just keeping the two carts up and running was my totality. To fill in my time between customers, I read magazines from the gift shop. South Carolina kept cropping up. I tucked such knowledge away. We were still living at the government subsidized San Rafael Apartments. The apartments are still there.

Getting burned out, I decided to sell the Eldorado Hotel cart and I asked one of our helpers if she would like to buy it. She said yes. I sold it to her for the same amount the bank loaned me to buy it and she changed the name to Bean Queen. She took ownership July 1st, 1994.

This left us with just the mall cart. True, I wasn't working a hundred hours a week anymore but I was still working seven days a week. This was getting tiresome. I was tired of working in the mall.

Time to throw in the towel. Remember the kid I fired and his friend went with him? Well, I sold the cart to that friend's parents. Not exactly sure how that came about, but it did. Got the money I asked for. Because I was so burned out it didn't bother me to sell that which I put so much work into. The sale took place September 1st, 1994. I have a wandering spirit and decided to move to, you guessed it, South Carolina. Helen agreed to the move.

It was U-Haul time again, this time pulling our Honda Acura in back of the U-Haul. South Carolina, here we come. Can't exactly remember why but we chose Summerville, not too far from Charleston, but we did. As interesting as making espresso in Santa Fe was, the next year in Summerville would be, for some strange reason, the best year of my life. After spending a year in Summerville, we would move up to Whitehall, New York for about sixteen months, before moving back to Santa Fe. But I'm getting ahead of myself. Now, for the interesting part.

We found a place to live, a sorta kinda nice apartment complex. After unloading everything and returning the U-Haul, it was time to find a job. Within walking distance I got a job at Mr. K's Piggly Wiggly. Yes, Monday thru Friday, I was a grocery clerk. Shucks, and I thought Santa Fe was weird. This was sure different, but I loved it. Didn't have to run my own business anymore, with all the responsibility of running one's own business. All I had to do was walk to work and bag groceries. Granted, it only paid five dollars an hour, but at least I was happy. Obviously, I'm a people person, so meeting all these nice folks from Summerville was intriguing. I got along well with the Blacks, one customer even tipping me fifty dollars, even tho she was poor. I enjoyed carrying out their groceries to their car. I got along better with the Blacks than the Whites. One of the butchers was as skinny as a rail. Every day he would buy a six pack of Budweiser to take home with him and I think that's all he lived on. It wasn't long before I got pulled over for speeding and had to stand in front of the judge alongside the police officer who pulled me over. Didn't get out of this one and had to pay the fine. The South isn't like Seattle and it certainly isn't like Santa Fe. These are down home folk with simple lives and a lot of them are government subsidized.

Summerville is a dual community. On one side of the street are shacky homes and on the other side of the street are mansions. I don't have to tell which people lived in which. Sad to say, racism is alive and sick in the South. I would go to a party and the N word was commonly used by the White folk. This was disturbing to me. To numb the pain, I drank at one party some Burgermeister. But the host of the party eventually asked me to leave because I was hitting on his girlfriend. That's what Burgermeister will do to you. Got lost going home but I finally made it home safely. Again, not for the faint of heart.

There was a German couple who came in regularly to Piggly Wiggly and, in conversation, told me they had a bike for sale. This was an interesting bike, insomuch as it was made in Italy, a one speed, and folded up. I believe it was invented for urban transportation. Here's the cool part: I installed a bike seat on the back and every Friday after work I would put Boaz, now two, in the bike seat and we would ride around the neighborhood. The Black folk would be holding their barbecues in the back yard. We would wave to each other as we rode by. I think they liked Boaz. Once, while riding thru a neighborhood, we were surrounded by thirty or forty black kids on the street. Not a problem: we took it low and slow as I walked the bike thru them and a lot of the kids tapped Boaz on his helmet in a friendly way.

There was a grocery store in Summerville, I think it's called Mystery Grocery. Quite small, and walking into it was like walking into the past. Screen door, wooden floor, old time refrigerators and freezers. Off on the side was a pool room. The Black folk let us in and Boaz loved it. He enjoyed all the colored balls and would laugh whenever one was hit.

Railroad tracks were nearby and we would wait for the 5:30 train to go by. The conductor would wave to Boaz. There was a lumber yard, also nearby, and Boaz was awed at the heavy machinery. Kids like that sort of stuff.

Helen and I would do a little traveling, like Folly Beach or Charleston. The ocean was refreshing. We also enjoyed walking around Charleston, admiring the skinny row houses. That's where we learned that Charleston green is nine parts black and one part green. Those houses made us want to live there. But alas, the humidity was too much. I would be standing in a parking lot, standing still, and the sweat would be dripping off of me. I just couldn't take the humidity. We decided to take a vacation and drove up to Whitehall, New York, where my brother lived. Liked it so much that we decided to move there. At least this time, I knew someone at my destination. U-Haul time again. Of course we ran out of gas on the way up. A nice highway patrol man drove me to a gas station and back to the U-Haul with gas. I love our highway patrol.

My brother is an auctioneer in Whitehall, New York and he was kind enough to put me to work for him. He would be summoned to different houses to clear them out for auctioning. It was interesting to see all the different paraphernalia old houses in upstate New York had to offer. During auctioning, when I was helping him, every now and then I would bid on an item. One particular item got away from me. He told me who got the winning bid and told me where he lived. I went to his house and asked him if he would sell me the item. He did. It's an old Jewish school desk. I know it's Jewish because of the Star of David on the inkwell cover. We use it in our house to this day.

Remember that young woman who worked the gift shop back at the Eldorado Hotel? Well, she moved to Vermont so one Sunday I drove over to see her. She didn't want to be seen by me. I felt rejected, all for the better I suppose. So I drove to a liquor store, picked up a half pint of whiskey and drove the back roads of Vermont with the window down. I was all alone on the roads and the scenery was very beautiful, actually. Quite peaceful on a Sunday morning.

But I was getting depressed in New York because here I was, an excellent barista and not able to find a decent job. Sometimes I would take Boaz to the local library, which was an old house. Each time, I would read to Boaz a certain book, My Great Aunt Arizona, a children's book. I loved that book. When we would get back to Santa Fe, I couldn't find the book in the children's section of our library. I petitioned the library to obtain this book and they agreed. Thanks to me, you can now (probably) find this book in the library in the children's section in Santa Fe.

Needing more income, I became a garbage man for three weeks, serving the community of Lake George. Garbage men are gods to kids and I loved it. Then I became one of the managers for a coffee shop in Rutland, Vermont. In my off time we would walk around the Rutland Cemetery which has huge oak trees. We collected acorns off the ground, all of which are now in a jar in our house. Anyway, the main manager of the coffee shop was a mean, mean man. Nonetheless, I got along quite well with a customer and one of the employees. And yes we kissed. That's all I'll say about that. Only to say that twenty years later, back in Santa Fe, a customer came into the shop who knew him and totally understood his being mean and my leaving him. I told this customer that I got my revenge by being a successful and happy barista. Anyway, after six months at the coffee shop, I quit. Then I worked in a Norton factory. Norton is a French conglomerate with over a thousand factories in the United States and Mexico. You may see the Norton name at your hardware store. It was a second shift job. It was boring but it was money. Then, one night, while working at a machine, I got a vision, and at the end of the vision, I heard an inward voice: call the woman who had bought your cart and ask her if you can buy your cart back. So the next day I called her and left a message to call me back. This was December 12th, 1996. A few days later she called me and I asked her if I could buy my cart back. She said yes.

This was cool. Now all I had to do was the U-Haul thing again. Did I tell you? While living in Whitehall we bought a

1961 Chevy step van with the hopes of converting it into a coffee truck to sell espresso in Santa Fe. This meant renting a trailer, along with the U-Haul, and pulling that van behind the U-Haul, all the way to Santa Fe. Talk about scary! I don't advise it. Now in January 1997, we stayed our first night in Santa Fe in a hotel. Unfortunately, it was quite cold that night and our little espresso maker, in the U-Haul, froze and broke. The idea of selling espresso out of that step van didn't pan out so I sold it a few months hence.

Before we left New York, we asked the woman who was co-working Bean Queen Espresso to scout around for a place to live. She found a mobile home just south of Española along the side of the road. The heating vents on the floor in the kitchen had no grates and, apparently, mice fell into the vents and died, so that every time we turned on the heater, we smelled dead mice. We brought this to the attention of the landlord and all he did was give us an air freshener. How nice. Anyway, living just south of Española meant traveling Highway 285 to get to work. Rough commute but I didn't mind: I was back in New Mexico and I had my old cart back. Meanwhile, Helen and I opened a smaller espresso cart at Outside Magazine. That gig didn't last that long but I suppose it was fun.

One thing I suppose I should mention is, we wanted to change the name from Bill's Espresso to something else. While getting ready in January 1997, Helen and I brainstormed for a new name. After about twenty possibilities, we chose Holy Spirit Espresso because when it came out of my mouth the words just rolled off my tongue. We eliminated the other possibilities and made our choice. We thought, well, the name may be a bit controversial, but after all, Santa Fe means Holy Faith and we knew we could get away with it. After all the prep work, we opened up February 1st, 1997 at the Eldorado Hotel.

We were able to sell espresso at Hotel Santa Fe with that smaller cart after Outside Magazine. Once again, that gig didn't last long. One day, a fellow said he would buy the cart if could deliver it to his brother who owned a coffee shop on

Wickenden Street in Rhode Island. I said sure! So I rented a van, loaded the cart into the van, and Boaz and I drove to Rhode Island. I delivered the cart the brother and he gave me files to bring back to Santa Fe. Okay, I can do this. On our way back, I decided to drive down to Florida to visit my parents. When it came time to leave, I only had twenty-five hours to get the van back to Santa Fe so drove nonstop. Well, having driven thru two time zones, I'm the only guy I know who drove twenty-seven hours in twenty-five hours time.

The manager of the Eldorado Hotel went on to become the general manager of Hotel Santa Fe and the Eldorado Hotel now has a new general manager. Maybe we got along okay. I didn't bother him and he didn't bother me. So long as I paid my rent on time, everything was okay. The convenience was my getting my milk from their kitchen. Didn't have to get my milk from a store anymore.

We left that mobile home along the side of the highway just south of Española, along with its smelly mice, and we're renting a house at 824 Agua Fria Street, close enough to the Eldorado Hotel to where I could ride my bicycle to work. Y'know, that Italian bicycle I bought back in Summerville that I would ride Boaz around in. The house had a small back yard which made for good family time. The house also had mice. Using mouse traps, I caught about a dozen mice, put them in a bag and took the bag to the landlord, dropped that bag of mice on the agent's desk, opened the bag, showed her, and said point blank, do something about this!

I would set the cart up by seven in the morning, then I'd go for a walk around downtown Santa Fe before I opened up at eight. First I would walk to the Federal Courthouse where Billy the Kid was arraigned and I would sit on the steps and smoke a cigarette. Then I walked up to the Loretto Chapel and picked up cigarette butts off the premises. Part of my duty to Santa Fe, I guess.

I remember a Renta Yenta from New York City one morning who demanded I sell her my last New York Times. Of course she didn't have any sway on me while her husband stood by her side, silent as could be. He knew better.

Anyway, for the first time, I found myself fitting into Santa Fe with a sense of belonging. Let the good times roll. With the two women filling in for me every now and again, I could begin focusing on my customers. Customers were far and few between. That New York depression started setting in again. Nonetheless, I stayed focused on what few customers I was getting. Like the couple who was staying at the hotel for a few nights and came down every morning. The lady made note that I was the first barista who made it a point to put the lid on her husband's stainless steel coffee mug properly with the lid opening properly facing him. On Friday nights I would occasion myself at El Paseo for a beer. Small compensation for a lack of customers but hey, I was back in Santa Fe. Or how about the important man with a big SUV who ordered his latte with the phone to his ear and paid with a hundred dollar bill. Not a problem. I gave him his change with a thumbs up, got a dollar tip, and sent him on his way. Being dysfunctional, I didn't mind sacrificing myself for the benefit of others.

Here are some of my customers. National Guardsmen showed up, staying at the hotel, all trim and handsome. Good to serve them. Two women from Holland enjoyed my cappuccinos and remarked about the intense silence of our Southwest. The next week a well dressed group with suits and ties arrived and what impressed me so much was how well behaved they were. As if they were all tied to rules and regulations. Not at all like me. Not at all like the couple who showed up the next day and we just chatted and chatted, having a good time. How about a bunch of guys from the East Coast who wore black and didn't know how to say hi or smile. Belgian customers seem to have been the best because they carried an exuberance with them. Or a family of five who were staying at the hotel for a few nights. I'll never forget them. They loved each other with constant conversation: carefree, fearless, shameless, interactive and close to each other. The perfect all-American family. I had a sign out front ("Best coffee in Santa Fe") and a customer told me that his grandfather told him that rare is an advertisement that lives up to its name. That made my day.

An easy to talk to man from American Express told me that a sense of humor was essential to longevity. I think he was the vice president. A man from Amsterdam for a radiology convention bought a latte and exclaimed that his latte was unbelievably excellent.

One day a strange man comes to the cart wearing thick glasses pressed against his thick black eyebrows. He worked for the Department of Transportation and was waiting for his Los Alamos rendezvous. He eventually orders two drinks. Not being socially minded, not the type of guy who got out much, he was asked to leave the hotel and wait outside for his ride.

I truly enjoyed good conversationalists who were open and free to talk with me. A rarity. So it was pleasant when one day a couple showed up and for the few minutes we were together, we laughed and laughed. Then they left and it was back to being slow again. It's amazing how depressing depression can be when it's slow. But enough about that.

The security guard at the hotel and I got along well together. He would stop by every day and ask how things were. He didn't reveal his work to me but he did tell me the story of a man who tried to pull a slip-and-fall on the hotel but the security camera found him out.

Government officials would stay at the hotel because of the elaborate security system in place. Can you say Ruth Bader Ginsburg? Or a vice president. I would always know when someone important was staying at the hotel because of the black SUV out front with a dozen antennas sticking out of its roof, along with all the security guards out front and on the roof of the hotel, Not to mention my espresso cart being inspected. But I'll say this: I saw a lot of security from around the world when their dignitaries would stay at the hotel and America's security folk are the best. Gosh darn handsome and they excel in PR. Professional yet friendly.

A former governor would stop by the hotel every now and again, and when he did, would stop by the cart. Nice guy.

A few famous people showed up at my cart. Joe Montana, Grace Slick, Tony Hawk, the lead singer of Rush (who came down every morning with his body guard and we would talk), and movie stars who wanted to remain incognito. Hotel employees would say, "Do you know who that was?" No. Like actors from the movie "Dances With Wolves," etc. I asked a Native American who was in the movie "Dances With Wolves" which roles he liked the most. He told me "the ones that pay the most." One day two women, one dressed in black and one dressed in white, who called themselves salt and pepper, invited me up to their room. I said no.

The Eldorado Hotel had a restaurant called The Old House, which is where I did my dishes at the end of the day. I became friends with the chefs. They told me the proper way to roast a turkey. These days, I smoke a turkey outside in the smoker, about four times a year. It's an all day affair but I get to sip a beer in the process.

One day I hugged three customers. Or should I say, three customers hugged me. Not the insulting shoulder hugs mind you, but the full frontal close and lingering kind of hug. They appreciated me and my product and I appreciated them and their hugs.

By now, our three women helpers had moved on to other things. This leaves Helen and I alone to run the cart, although we did have a part time employee. Just by observing how he treated customers changed my life. I believe he was a saxophone player. He was always happy and conscientious. His customers loved him. He taught me how to be nice to my customers. How did he do it? Always nice! I purposed my presentation to be like him. He was always friendly to his customers. Once he left, I did the weekdays and Helen worked the weekends. Still not making much money but we're happy. Actually, we're in debt. This bothered me because even tho I'm making excellent espresso, better than anyone else, my excellent customers are far and few between. It's depressing to make the best lattes around and there's nobody around to buy them.

At this point in time, settling in to my comfort zone, I was able to focus in on my customers. Customers from all over the world, staying at the hotel, who loved my coffee. How about the young woman who was tall and slender with a well worn look. How about the two women from Holland who enjoyed chatting with me. Or the cowboy with whiskey on his breath and an Oriental woman at his side. I was determined to keep on keeping on, as they say. Whoever they are. I enjoyed two sisters whenever they came to the cart together. Or the man with a cane, as if wounded in the line of duty.

Even tho business is slow, the days are warming up and pretty soon I was outside underneath the portale. Way cool on a warm morning. Morning time at the Eldorado Hotel was paradise. I hung a bird feeder up about ten feet from the cart and the birds would keep me entertained. Vehicular traffic was slow, Santa Fe was starting to wake up and the shadows on the Hilton Hotel across the street made the ambience heavenly. Yes, may I say it: a piece of Heaven on earth. As I was fond of saying, everything but the ocean.

Or how about the woman who owned goats. She was down to earth. Then there's the butler at the hotel and the stories he would tell. He was always doing this and going there for hotel guests. He ordered double espressos and wanted me and would always say "Someday, upstairs." He liked Boaz. Unfortunately, when the new general manager of the hotel came on, things changed. I don't know if this had anything to do with it, but the butler, at home, fell off a ladder, hit his head, and died. That took the wind out of our sails.

Then there was a simple woman with pig tails who amazed me because she was, in a way, so simple. I took her picture which is in the photo album. Yes, you should see it. Anyway, she came to Santa Fe for a margarita. Being Mr. Hospitality, I obliged. On that scooter, the two of us, riding down Cerrillos Road, with a store bought margarita (sorry), went to her hotel room on Cerrillos Road. And yes, we kissed. It's not a good idea to ride Cerrillos Road with two on a scooter, during rush hour, but we did it. More on the scooter later.

Or the well dressed man who visited my cart several mornings. He was generous with his spirit, generous with his tips, and politely generous with his beautiful wife.

Here's an interesting story. A middle aged Christian man, too poor to own a car, always rode a bicycle and was a friendly customer, stood outside my window at the Eldorado Hotel, speaking for fifteen minutes with an incredibly well dressed Jewish man. I'd give anything to have heard their conversation.

More people: a couple on their way to Seattle stopped off in Santa Fe to get married. Or the world traveler who carried his money, coins and all, in a bag. Or the three kids showing up in the morning who were up all night on peyote. Or the cute couple from Oklahoma. Or the woman who just got back from touring France and barely tipped a quarter. Or the women from Texas, dressed to the nines, smelling good. Their sugar daddy, standing by their side, was ruggedly handsome.

The Eldorado Hotel is a convention hotel. I always enjoyed a good convention, i.e., friendly environment and good tippers. One convention had two standouts: the woman who acts like she's seen it all and another one who acts like she's done it all. We talked and laughed whenever they came to the cart during breaks.

A peculiar note: while at the Eldorado Hotel I wore a baseball cap at work. This was getting too hot when I was inside. Big change: On January 1st, 2000, I began the tradition of wearing a bandana. That tradition continued until my last day at work. And it was on January 1st, 2009, that I began wearing a neckerchief. That tradition also lasted until my last day at work. I own over a hundred handkerchiefs. I was given the name Bandana Bill.

A well known and community-minded woman owns a bookstore on a street near where I'm set up. She asked me that if I ever moved, would I like to set up my cart at her place. Unfortunately, I couldn't, so I said no.

Postcard time, a bit of history. And this is sort of important. I left my mom and dad in Rockford, Illinois in January 1975 to attend Phoenix College so I could become a disc jockey. One day, I had fifteen cents in my pocket. Poor college student and decision time. I could either buy a candy bar for myself or buy a postcard from the post office and send it off to my dad.

I decided on the latter. Dad said he got more pleasure out of that postcard than I could have gotten out of that candy bar. From that day forward, while attending Phoenix College to become a disc jockey, I sent over a thousand postcards to mom and dad, usually on a daily basis, just to keep in touch with them. To this day, in doing my part to keep the post office in business, I still send out postcards regularly.

Anyway, from Phoenix, back to the future. It's 1998 and a regular county employee who always tipped with a two dollar bill, said he was going to Italy and asked if he could bring back anything. Me, being Mr. Postcard, told him to just send me a postcard. This started the ball rolling. From then on, whenever a regular told me they weren't going to see me for a couple of weeks because they were going on vacation, I asked them to send me a postcard. I began to receive postcards. Then, the tourists wanted to get in on the act and would send me a postcard when they got back home. Sometimes even before they got back home.

Little by little, postcards began arriving. I love postcards. I displayed all the post cards I received on the front of my espresso cart. Half from locals and half from tourists. Over five hundred postcards of fan mail from all over the world. Santa Fe attracts people from all over the world. And Santa Fe locals travel all over the world.

Now for me: There was a prominent woman who wanted to cut in line whenever she came to the cart at the Eldorado Hotel. I told her no and she complained to the manager who called me on the carpet. He told me I had to treat people like her differently because of their status in society. She once told me I needed a brochure holder on my cart to hold any brochures she might want to give me and that she would pay for it. I got the stand but she didn't pay for it. Then she said I needed an umbrella for my cart, like the umbrellas in the courtyard, and she would pay for it. I got the umbrella, like those in the courtyard, but again, she didn't pay for it.

Then there was this other woman, a hotel employee. We were good friends until she wrote a three page letter to the hotel manager full of lies about me, which was read out loud to me in his office with her sitting next to me. I had to sit there, in his office, listening to her lies. That depressed me. But again, I had to keep on keeping on. I was just glad not to be kicked off the property. He had every right to since I wasn't under any contract. I guess now is a good enough time as any to mention the food and beverage manager. She liked me and once told me that if the hotel manager didn't like me I wouldn't be around. Once, when I was waiting in the hotel lounge for Helen, she bought me a drink from the bar. Nice lady.

Being the wild child that I am, I thought it wise to begin behaving myself. I loved my customers tho, maybe a little bit too much. One woman, looking to get even with her soon-to-be ex-husband and living in Los Angeles, invited me over to her casita where she was staying. After a bottle of wine outside on the street side patio, we went into her room and yes, we kissed.

Or this new age woman who invited me up to her room. I think she wanted me to become a new ager like herself, going so far as to put candles and whatnot on a table in front of the entrance way to the rooftop balcony. I had to step over this table to get to the rooftop balcony. When we got back into the room, we sat on the bed. That's all. And yes, we kissed.

It was now 1998 and I wanted a camera to take pictures of my customers. I got a hold of a company magazine out of New York City and eventually talked to a salesman. iPhones weren't invented yet so in between customers I had to leave the cart, walk down the hallway in the hotel and use a pay phone every time I wanted to talk to him. This was starting to get expensive but, being persistent, I kept talking to him and, eventually, I got the camera I wanted, a Contax, that was small and portable. Why I didn't use a camera shop in Santa Fe to buy a camera, I don't know. Guess I do things the hard way. Anyway, for the next five years, I took photographs of my customers, both tourists and locals, mainly black and white photos. So I now have a five-year photo album of a lot of my customers. You should see it.

Sad time: Helen and I, with Boaz, went to the state fair in Albuquerque in 2003 and I left the camera behind on a seat. I lost my camera. Oh how I wailed and cried. I had lost my life. Never got the camera back and I was so distraught that, instead of buying another camera, I just gave up taking pictures altogether. Still got the photo album tho.

Unfortunately, Starbucks moved in up the street and my income was cut in half. We're now living next door to povertyville. Nevertheless, Helen and I managed to tailgate once a week. It's like this: At this time we were driving the Honda Element. We would throw a blanket in the back, pick up a bottle of wine, order take-out with a coupon from either Pyramid Cafe or the Santa Fe Baking Company and drive up to the National Cemetery and park in our usual spot facing the back of the tombstones where the spouse's names were printed. Then we would open up the back and enjoy our picnic. We did this every Friday for fifteen years.

One day we received a letter in the mail telling us we had thirty days to move out of the house we were renting on Agua Fria. What were we to do but move. We found an apartment over on Camino Carlos Rey. A little further away but we had a place to stay. Since this was further away, I needed some transportation, so I bought a scooter. A cheap Made in China scooter. I knew things were bad when I couldn't even start the thing on the first day I owned it. Only had that thing for six months before I finally gave up on that thing and walked it back to the dealer I bought it from and said, "Here, you can have this piece of junk." Then I walked away.

Here's the miracle part as mentioned in the forward. Time to get serious. It is now 1999 and Helen and I wanted to buy a house. Three of my customers, who always arrived together, worked for a bank. These three helped me obtain a loan to buy our house. Since I owned my own business, the bank wanted two years of my tax returns. These three greased the skids, helped me with the paperwork, vouched for me and, in the end, got us a loan to buy a house.

Here's a cool part I think you'll like. At the time, the Santa Fe Community Housing Trust had a program where, if you take their six week program, you'll be given a $15,000 loan as a down payment, to be paid back when you sell your house, to buy your house. A great guy headed the classes. He, again, greased the skids to smooth the way to getting us the down payment to buy the property and the house. As a result, I gave him a lifetime guarantee of getting free coffee. I honestly think, if not for him, we wouldn't be living in the house we're living in.

Now, on to another fellow who helped us. I just don't know what I would have done without him. So begins a great relationship. At this point in time, my La Marzocco espresso machine was beginning to nickel and dime me. God bless La Marzocco but their espresso machines don't last forever. So what does? Whenever I had a problem, though, I knew my new friend knew exactly what to do. Such as, "Bill, you need a new relief valve." So it's Friday before a busy three day weekend and I need a new relief valve. That's a ninety dollars next day delivery charge, but at least I got my new relief valve. My expert walked me through the installation. Then he tells me I need to clean out my machine. Okay, I can do this. I took the entire La Marzocco espresso machine apart, drove it down to the local car wash, flushed the tank out with the power house, drove the machine back to the hotel, put it all back together, and made it work. It worked. But then again, nickel and dime time. Whenever something went wrong, I knew I could call for help and would be told what to do. Lordy! This guy was such a business saver.

He liked me and was always willing to help me. Anyway, he retired and I wanted to send him a thank you letter, only to find out that he had died and I never got to send that a thank you letter for all the work he had done for me. It's a regret I have to live with for the rest of my life.

Back to the house. Actually, we bought one and a half acres about two miles from the Eldorado Hotel. This meant a lot of work. Here's a naked piece of land which we now own. So where do we get the house? Who's going to level the land on which the house is going to sit? What about electricity? What about a telephone cable? Who's going to drill the well? And once the well is drilled, how do we get water to the house? How about the septic system? Where do I get propane and how do I hook it up to the house? What about the driveway? What about the slope analysis? Who's gonna do the driveway? What about the necessary permits? I'm naive at this and this is not going to be easy.

Remember my health inspector? Here's how he now plays into the picture. He now works for the New Mexico Health Department and he told me where to put the septic system and how far the well had to be from our septic tank system. His coworker, born in Africa, shows us where the well can be placed. Apparently, there's a huge aquifer underneath our property that extends for miles. Anyway, that's what we tapped into. This well water plays an integral part in our business. As you will find out.

So I'm running this little espresso cart at the Eldorado Hotel, we got the property, and now, where to get the house. Well, there was a company in Albuquerque that built homes and then drove these houses to the property. It takes four months for the house to be built and once a month we would drive down to Albuquerque to inspect the house and give our approval. I should tell you that at the Eldorado Hotel was a real estate firm and one of their employees, when he ordered a drink, would immediately walk away from the cart. I mean, everyone else sticks around and converses. Not him. Anyway, he was the one who told me about this company and how we could get a house on the cheap.

Trying to put a house on a piece of property doesn't come easy. Again, we keep on keeping on and we don't give up. Our well was dug 480 feet down. One guy put in our septic system, the water line from the well to the house was dug by somebody, complete with beer cans left on the property, the electricity pole has been placed and electricity has been run from the street to the pole, complete with fuse box and meter, and the telephone cable from the street has been laid. I hate having to be my own contractor in a strange town, having never done this before, all the while running an espresso cart. Everything had to be done in order and if something goes wrong, it creates a domino effect. Like when the man who was supposed to install the electricity pole got into an accident with his equipment truck and couldn't install the pole for another week. Or the man who broke the water line from the well to the house, putting dirt in our faucets, and the water line had to be repaired. Or the cable box out front got water in it and had to be repaired. Ben was my go between with City Hall to get my slope analysis approved from an existing slope analysis. It's been said by chefs that the devil is in the details and it's true when putting everything together for a house on a piece of property.

And let me tell you about dealing with City Hall and getting all the necessary permits. Y'know, the same ones who lied to me about setting up an espresso cart? Well, my main contact in dealing with the city had a voicemail that was full. This meant, while Helen ran the espresso cart at the Eldorado Hotel in between home schooling Boaz, I was showing up at City Hall and waiting for my City Hall contact to show up. But wait, there's more. He lost the paperwork! And I lost two weeks of time to get final approval for the house. But finally the building permit was, don't you know, found! Over the years, I have heard similar stories. That's just the way it is in Santa Fe.

Side note here: Since Helen and I were always poor, our dates in Seattle consisted of walking around neighborhoods. Hey, it's free. Two things we always wanted while looking at houses was, when we eventually got a house of our own: a long driveway and a screen door. In a sense, I had to be my own contractor. Not exactly an easy thing to do in a town like Santa Fe, especially since I had never done anything like this before. And all the while running a silly little espresso cart at a hotel.

Getting back to the long driveway. Our driveway was invented by teenage drinkers who used our property before it became our property to have their drinking parties. Broken bottles everywhere! Nevertheless, our long driveway came into being because of them. We just followed the driveway they made. We had a couple of culverts put in and completed the driveway up to the house. To this day, we still come across broken glass on the property here and there, especially after a good rain. As for the screen door, we bought one at Home Depot and it still works well to this day.

Our son is now a Green Beret in Special Forces. Boaz and I are not at all alike but we love each other. Boaz is highly disciplined and I'm a woo-hoo type of guy. But we go the distance, it's in our DNA. Which is why, when you get to the end of this book, you will see that I went the distance.

Speaking of our son: y'know, the one who was in the baby pack while I made espresso, was home schooled all twelve years by Helen. I ran the espresso cart and Helen taught Boaz. One car, one income, one house, one kid. I've been chastised before about saying this but here goes: I slept with my son's teacher!

And here comes a strange part. Since our house was built offsite it had to be trucked up to Santa Fe. Takes four hours. Do you know what it's like to see your house coming down the road to your property? It's a weird site to see. But wait, there's more. Santa Fe had a heavy rain the day before and the house, on the trailer, got stuck on the driveway. What to do. We called for a heavy duty Caterpillar tractor and had the house pulled up to the foundation. It only cost us four hundred dollars. After the house was placed on the foundation, the driver and I smoked a cigarette. This was the perfect culmination to finally getting our house. The miracle was over. Helen, Boaz and I slept our first night in our new house March 1st, 2001, on the floor.

When we moved into our house we didn't have a garage. How un-American! It wasn't until Helen and I lived in our house for two years that we finally had a garage built.

U-Haul time again. Time to pack everything up from our apartment on Camino Carlos Rey and drive across town to our new house. As we were driving away, Ray Charles was playing on the radio, "Hit the road, Jack, and don't you come back no more..." After all these years, we're still living in this house.

Our first weekends at our house were spent outside fixing up the property. Quite therapeutic to be working on one's own property. Moving rocks (oh, the rocks!), clearing brush, trimming trees, the usual smorgasbord of yard work. But oh, the joy of owning, for the first time, after decades of marriage, our own property and house, was indeed liberating. A young woman once came into the shop (more about the shop later) and I told her that two of the best pleasures of living in America is owning one's own business and owning one's own house. There is no substitute for freedom. My mission statement for the business was to live close enough to work so I could ride a bicycle to work. This is what I now started doing every day.

Today, on our property, are six rock walls I have built, all the while working the cart. More on that later, but I began building these walls in the summer of 2001. On a side note, it was during the summer of 2001 when two men from Hotel Plaza Real stopped by my cart. More about them later.

I'm going to tell you an interesting story. Helen, Boaz and I attended a wedding in Omaha, Nebraska in May, 2001. Driving back, we drove thru Kansas. We drove thru Great Bend. Upon entering Great Bend, there is a sign: Birthplace of Jack Kilbey. You may not know who Jack Kilbey is but, along with Robert Noyce, he revolutionized your life. Anyway, I had a customer who once lived in Great Bend and hated it so much that he moved away. I, on the other hand, was totally enthralled with Great Bend and Kansas. I thought Kansas was so cool and that this was the epitome of civilization. So much so, that, if we had not just moved into our house a few months earlier, I would have, with Helen and Boaz, moved to Kansas. Helen and Boaz were bored, slept in the car, while I videotaped Kansas while driving. Over the years, after that, I told many of my customers that if Dorothy was from any other state, she would have stayed in Oz.

After 9-11 and air travel was grounded, travelers in the hotel couldn't leave so I had a captive audience. Now for the moment. About a week later, a New York City firefighter stayed at the hotel for a few days. I figured he was in Santa Fe just to get away. He wore his FDNY cap. Every morning he would visit my cart and instead of ordering on the side like everyone else, he ordered in front of me on the other side of the espresso machine. That's cool. We conversed a little. Then he told me that today was his last day and he would be going back to New York City. As I passed his latte to him and we were both holding the cup, I hesitated and said to him, "Thank you." He sincerely looked at me, both of us still holding the cup and said "Thank you." A little bit of gratefulness, solace and comfort from Holy Spirit Espresso.

Now for the interesting part. Every year, at the Eldorado Hotel, there's an Oil and Gas Convention. It's now November 2001. It's seven in the morning, I'm at my espresso cart, and this handsome man comes to my cart and orders a 16 ounce latte. Just to make conversation, I asked him what he did for a living. OMG moment: He said, "I'm the Governor of Kansas." Wow! At this point in time, he's my Second Coming! I raved and raved how much I loved Kansas. Later in the year, he sent us a Christmas card. I love this guy. Maybe we'll meet again someday.

Around this time, a fellow who worked across the street, Mike, approached me at the Eldorado Hotel and said he had the perfect spot for my cart. He showed me this hole in the wall across the street, 6x8, which used to be the small lobby for those who used the elevator which was now taken out of service. I politely told him no, thinking, "You will never, ever get me into that spot." That was a mistake I made. Would have saved me a whole lot of trouble, as you will soon find out.

Now for the hard part. The hotel changed. The gift shop was gone, along with all the shops down the hall, to set up a spa. Also gone was a woman who worked in one of those shops. And yes, we kissed. I'm now, with my espresso cart, pushed outside. Outside into the cold. I had to beg the hotel to give me a couple of heat lamps just to keep me warm outside in the cold. One morning it was below zero and my coffee maker stopped working and my espresso machine froze up. The steaming wands froze up. I had to close up shop and go home that day. Do you know anyone who has tried to make espresso outside when it's below zero? I do.

I was so depressed. Most of the time I was just standing around, not getting much business. I was cranky and bored. Sure, I was selling excellent espresso, but where are my customers? I know, they're going up the street. They don't even know what they're missing. On top of that, it's allergy season and I feel miserable. I'm crying every day but I'll say this: at least every customer I get is a quality customer and I delivered a quality product with quality service.

Things, believe it or not, were about to get worse. The hotel was now sold to another corporation. This meant a new general manager who didn't like me. He pushed me to the side of the hotel. If not for the support of the community, he would have gotten rid of me altogether.

Actually, first I was put in a hallway at the other end of the hotel. Not much business. Still going further in debt. But I made too much noise so I was put in what was then the courtyard. But now I was in the way of events so I was now pushed to the side of the hotel in the breezeway. It ain't called a breezeway for nothing. Oh so cold and windy. I could be wrong on this but I believe the January and February of 2003 when I was outside were the wettest since Abraham Lincoln was president. Still dying every day. Still crying every day. I'm one of the best baristas in America and I'm living in poverty. Anyway, I think I was the laughing stock of the county employees who worked right next door to the hotel. Outside in the snow and rain for a whole year. Open at six every morning. This wasn't very much fun anymore. Sometimes I would forget to put the airpot underneath the coffee maker and all my coffee ended up on the floor. I wasn't very bright back then. Under depression and stress I guess. But the few county employees I got were excellent customers. One bright spot was during Indian Market. A lot of booths were set up in the courtyard and business boomed, if only for one weekend.

My drive-up customers had no place to park so they parked out front on the sidewalk. Then one day, while making a drink for a customer, this man walks up to my cart and shoves his badge in my face. He shouts at me and tells me that my customers cannot park on the sidewalk otherwise he will ticket them. Sort of embarrassing when I'm trying to be Mister Excellent Espresso Man for my customers and this intruder breaks into the party. Come to find out, he's the head honcho over all the parking police and he's not gonna take any guff. From that time on, I let my customers know not to park on the sidewalk.

Silver lining: As bad as it was trying to make a living on the side of the Eldorado Hotel, the view up Palace Avenue, looking east toward The Palace of the Governors where the Native Americans sell their goods in the morning, when the sun was rising, was priceless. Got pictures.

It wasn't long before I couldn't take it anymore. But I had a mortgage to pay. Argh! We left the Eldorado Hotel. I was now unemployed with no income so I approached The Santa Fe Art Museum on Palace Avenue and asked if I could set up my cart in their courtyard. They said yes. Unfortunately, there wasn't enough business to sustain us so we closed up shop after a couple of months. At the time, the manager of the Art Museum wanted me to give a discount for her employees. She was making good money and I'm struggling. Only stayed there for a couple of months.

Remember those two guys from Hotel Plaza Real? I approached them for permission to set up shop at their hotel and they said yes. I'm hoping this will work out. So I asked a good friend if he could transport my cart over to the hotel with his pick-up truck and he agreed. I opened up on January 2005 but was only there for six months. Sorta kinda had success but it's difficult when the hotel offers free coffee in the lobby. I think it was around this time that Hurricane Katrina hit New

Orleans and I overheard from a customer who lived there why New Orleans failed. Basically, it was because of a bunch of city rulers who probably couldn't run a grade school if they tried.

Some customers of note. One was a doctor who travelled a lot. One day, while sitting in a coffee shop in Dubai, he reads a little ditty about me in The New York Times. Go figure.

There was a doctor from Europe who spoke seven languages and drank his cappuccino with me every morning. The HMO director from back East who envied me and wished he could get out from underneath The Machine. The retired shareholder from California who had to be taught about tipping. And then there was "her," but I'm a married man.

A very pretty Black woman walks up to the cart, elderly and Hollywood style, complete with a handbag and gray hair. As polite as a queen, she orders a small black coffee, thanks me and walks away.

Or the man who grew up under a totalitarian regime in East Germany and was in the audience when President Reagan told Gorbachev, "Tear down this wall." He was in Santa Fe for a few days, a scientist for a vaccine convention. Then there's Dr. Feelgood. Can't remember his real name but he worked for the county and had a weekly radio program on the local radio. Dr. Feelgood was a cool dude and I always enjoyed him coming into the shop. And there were two guys, real estate agents, who would buy Boaz gifts.

Then one morning in spring, the hotel manager of Hotel Plaza Real, while vacationing in Tucson, called me and point blank told me to move my espresso cart outside. He was in sunny, warm Tucson and outside Hotel Plaza Real was horizontal blowing snow. Things were not going well at all. Again. But one morning a cool customer of sorts, came to the cart and his actions were, well, sorta funny. We both still remember that morning.

Here's a bright spot though: a woman, who used to work for Coffee Kids, was now teaching English to students in Guatemala. A few from her class flew up to Santa Fe with her so she could show them around. She brought this bunch to my cart and it was good conversing with them while they bought some coffee. When they got back home she had the whole class write me postcards. I received twenty-four of them.

Then one morning, the hotel owner told me that if I wasn't out of his hotel by the end of the day he would call the police. Nice guy. So I called up a friend again and he drove all of my equipment in his pick-up truck and we put everything in my garage. Time to look for a new place to set up shop.

It's now the summer of 2006 and nowhere to place our espresso cart, sitting in the garage, and I'm going further in debt. Desperate people do desperate things so out of desperation I called up Mike and asked him if that tiny hole in the wall was still available. He said yes. Okay, I'm desperate so I'll take it and I was thinking, I hope I don't regret this. So I called up my friend and asked him if he could help me move my espresso cart out of the garage and into that tiny space. He helped me move the espresso cart into that tiny space. I paid a thousand dollars to have the proper electricity installed. As I was setting up shop, sitting outside in my car in front of the shop, of course, I got a parking ticket.

In opening up the shop I received three parking tickets. Time to go to court again, only this time with Boaz. Since Boaz was homeschooled, this would be a lesson in how our judicial system worked. I told Boaz: Rome, in all of its barbarianism, allowed its citizens the right to appeal and that's what we're going to do. Appeal. Time to stand in front of the judge. Again. I pleaded my case, she listened and said case dismissed! I told Boaz, that's how democracy works.

The cart is now installed and I'm ready to begin business. The walls are naked and white, one fluorescent fixture on the ceiling, and the only thing I have on the wall is my eight and a half by eleven menu. The day is July 2 and my first customer was a guy who lived in Texas and visited Santa Fe regularly. Of course, that first dollar now hangs on the wall.

So begins the second half of my selling espresso in Santa Fe. This encapsulated about two years at Villa Linda Mall, two years at the Eldorado Hotel, two and a half years in the East, nine more years back at the Eldorado Hotel, a little bit at Outside Magazine, a little bit at the New Mexico Art Museum, a little bit at Hotel Santa Fe, and now this, a 6x8 hole-in-the-wall at 225 West San Francisco Street. The next fifteen years would prove to be quite interesting.

Honestly, this is sorta depressing. Every morning when my feet hit the floor I had to pump myself up. How did it get this bad? I'm an excellent barista doing an excellent job and now I'm stuck in this (sorry) hole-in-the-wall. How am I supposed to make my customers happy if I'm so sad? So pump myself up I did. Be positive! Be creative! Be innovative!

The outside of the shop was without furniture so Helen and I bought a table and four chairs, along with a red awning to go over the door. Eventually, I bought a sign, designed by my graphics designer and made by a local sign shop. Background? Red, of course. The place was coming together. I asked the owner of The Santa Fe New Mexican newspaper for some publicity. She granted my request, letting her readers know where Holy Spirit Espresso was now located. She was even kind enough to send a photographer over to the shop. Pictures are a newspaper's attraction.

Okay. So the outside is looking good, but not totally yet. I needed an umbrella. So I order an umbrella stand and an umbrella. Let's do Cinzano; after all, it's a universally known name, in movies no less, and easily recognizable. An attraction, especially since I'm attracting people from all over the world. The outside is looking good, now how about the inside of the shop.

Yeah, the walls are still bare, white no less, with that one fluorescent fixture on the ceiling. You know, that prison cell look. Even that jail look, where I've been in two states before. Anyway, time to decorate. I mean, the espresso is excellent, my drinks are excellent, but I need a shop that's inviting. You and I both know we've been in establishments where the decor is inviting but the product sends you out the door, never to come back. So I added a clock (clocks are good) and tacked up a calendar. Then I put up a small mirror, eye level of course, near the door. People like to look at themselves to make sure they're looking good. That mirror got a lot of use.

I needed pictures. Nothing expensive, just something to fill the space. Fortunately, I knew a woman who worked at the local library who donated to me magazines that were donated to the library. And yes, we kissed, but the last time we saw each other was at my favorite body shop. No play on words, please. So I'm beginning to get magazine pictures on my walls but my walls are still white. And that stupid fluorescent fixture on my ceiling in my tiny fifty square foot coffee shop is still an embarrassment.

Then one day, this man from California comes in and begins telling me about something. I really didn't know what he was talking about, but he said he would send it to me. I said okay. Well, don't you know, a couple of weeks later, whatever he was talking about arrived in the mail. Don't you know, he owns this company that makes really cool fluorescent light fixture covers. All right! The shop is looking cool.

But those terrible white walls. So I drove over to a hardware store that sold paint and gathered a bunch of color samples. I needed customer input as to what color to paint my walls. After a couple of weeks, we agreed on what color to paint the walls. I can do this! Take everything down off the walls, cover the machine, paint the walls, put all the pictures back up on the newly painted walls, and be happy with the results. Now, when my feet hit the cold floor in the morning, at least I had something to look forward to.

At this point in time, the Internet was beginning to give me business. Y'know, Yelp, Google, Trip Advisor, Urban Spoon, etc. Just in time for my coffee shop to be fixed up. The outside looked good, the inside looked good, my coffee tasted good, I was good to go. True, I was still losing business to that out-of-state coffee chain up the street, but at least I had some competition power to contend with. Cell phones were becoming more handy and more popular and I would see people googling me outside the shop and when they liked what they read about the shop they would come on in. That's when

I heard those words after they tasted my espresso, "Wow, you really are the best!" Like the man, a stranger, who walks into the shop, knows what he wants (double short latte), knows how to order it and after a little chit chat, he pays, tips, sips, and acknowledges what an excellent drink it was. Another satisfied customer.

More customers: I made one customer an excellent latte, sold him a Danish for a dollar (where else can you find a Danish in Santa Fe for a dollar at 7:15 in the morning) and he didn't even tip. Ungratefulness shows its ugly head every now and then. A woman walks into my shop and tells me she has dirt from Chimayo in one of my cups in her house. This fat old man comes in and orders an espresso for here and while doctoring up his espresso, he keeps making grunts and groans and eventually says Great! Then he leaves. Here's one: two women were such a wonderful couple who took a walk together every morning and on occasion would stop by my shop with their dog and order their coffee drinks. I loved them because they were able to make me feel like a real barista.

Or this woman who was staying at La Fonda and wanted her latte delivered to her on Thanksgiving morning. So after setting up at seven am and not having to open up until eight, I strapped her latte into the back of my scooter and, with a bunch of snow on the streets, scooted and slipped slided away up to her hotel room and delivered her latte. And yes, we kissed.

Hard time. There was handicap parking outside the shop. Unfortunately, the parking police had their office right across the street from the shop. They watched that handicap parking spot like a hawk. So when a customer pulled up front for a quick purchase, that customer got a five hundred dollar ticket. I complained to the City of Santa Fe to have that handicap parking spot moved to a different location. It worked and the handicap parking spot was moved to the front of the Lensic Theater. This happened on the same day our house got broken into. Tit for tat I guess. At least now my customers won't be getting five hundred dollar fines anymore. Then the City put a meter in its place, but that got stolen. Ha! Eventually, a twenty minute loading zone sign was erected and that worked out okay. Except when a Palestinian would park his huge pickup truck out front and leave it there for hours on end, preventing pull-ups from taking place. Oh, he would make me angry. But what really made me angry was when he wouldn't pay his bill and I had to walk into his shop up the street and yell at him, "Pay your bill!" But we always remained friends. He wore his gun on his hip (Wild West, right) and one day he and his cousin across the street fired their guns in the air because of each other. His cousin, I understand, went to jail on drug charges but he was able to keep his business.

Where did The Lensic Theater get its name? I believe a family moved to Santa Fe from Turkey in the 1800s and started buying up property in downtown Santa Fe. Lensic is an acronym for the first letter of the names of his six kids.

One day a regular walks in and says, "My four friends and I believe you to be the best coffee shop we've ever visited in all parts of America. You're the best!" Shucks, made my day. In the years I worked the shop, I told my customers that when it comes to brains, I got the short end of the stick but we always play the hand we're dealt and I made the most of it.

Santa Fe has a couple of outstanding markets on the Plaza every year, Spanish Market in July and Indian Market in August. Every month there are events held on the Plaza. Corvette show, Low Rider show, you name it. This brought in a little bit of business. Then there's the annual Wine and Chili Festival held in September, which hosted special events in the Eldorado Hotel courtyard. Free wine!

Back at the coffee shop. The world famous Indian Market was so big that Helen had to help me out. She would be out front and I would be inside. It was a twelve hour day weekend. We had customers we would see only once a year. The line was constantly out the door. One hundred thousand people would show up for Indian Market, held on the Plaza. Our coffee shop was just three blocks from the Plaza. We had to be well stocked on all supplies, including water. Understand, I had no running water, and every day I had to bring in my own water in those five gallon water containers. Here's the importance of our well at home. One reason our espresso tasted so good was because we used our well water, not city water. Remember Olympia Beer? Their slogan was "It's the water." So true with espresso, too. If you ever want to see millions of dollars exchange hands, come to Indian Market. One hundred years old. Tribes from all over America attend.

After Indian Market, nothing much happens. It's back to business as usual. That is, until Zozobra. What? You never heard of Zozobra? This original burning man was done in 1924 by the artist Will Shuster in his back yard. Now, imagine 60,000 people plus in Fort Marcy Park chanting burn him, burn him, burn him, until Old Man Doom and Gloom goes up in smoke. Boaz and I would attend yearly. Quite the spectacle. After the burning, Boaz and I would walk to the Plaza. I remember one year walking behind a mother with her two kids commenting on the Christians who were witnessing for Jesus, telling her kids to just ignore the little people. After watching the crowd, along with all the police, it was time to go home. Owning a coffee business, I had to get up early the next morning, cold floor and all, and it was back to business as usual, except for all the beer bottles lying around my shop. Where's my coffee!

Next weekend came our two annual parades, the Pet Parade on Saturday and, the next day, our Historical/Hysterical Parade on Sunday. The Pet Parade is cool because kids bring their pets, many dressed up, and if you want to bring your pet iguana, you can do that. too. You got a goat? Bring her along! The Historical/Hysterical Parade had everything. Politics, Sports, Clubs, you name it. If you got a cause, you're in. We did good coffee business. Lots of families, lots of people, lots of fun. These two parades were not to be missed (even though I had to because I worked). The parade route was close to the shop. It's all about Santa Fe. It's local and I enjoyed seeing all the locals enjoying themselves.

More about my customers:
Europeans know good espresso and they know how to

enjoy it. One day a foursome stopped in and ordered two double espressos and two cappuccinos, water on the side, of course. They sat outside underneath the Cinzano umbrella enjoying themselves. It was good seeing people enjoying my product and resting outside on the chairs. Europeans are good at that: they know how to rest. We Americans are more come and go. It was common for me to stand outside the shop when I didn't have any customers and watch the cars go by. One time this car drives by with the window rolled down and an ex-movie star driving the car shouts out to me, "Hey Bill!" She was a good customer.

While Santa Fe is a tourist town, it's also a convention town. And since I was in between the Hilton Hotel and the Eldorado Hotel, I got to see a lot of conventioneers. My favorite group, year after year, was the Wilderness Medicine Group. Extrovertive, friendly, outgoing and intelligent. I developed a yearly relationship with some of them. One was always nice to me and we liked each other. Another annual convention group was the plastic surgeons. We called them the boob doctors because they all had trophy wives.

On occasion, usually in the morning, I would have to kick a jerk out of my shop. The kind of guy who stayed up all night and thought he had the right to take liberties in my shop. Gimme this and gimme that. On one occasion, this trouble maker was giving me a hard time and I didn't know what to do. Lucky for me, the retired Navy Seal who visited about once a year, happened to be sitting outside with his wife, the retired CIA agent. He helped me get rid of the kook. On another occasion, I was out on the sidewalk yelling at the top of my lungs at someone I just got finished kicking out of my shop, telling him not to come back. A store owner a few doors up heard me from inside his shop came out and asked me what that was all about. Oh, nothing unusual I told him. Or another time when this couple ordered an expensive drink, they left the shop while I was making their drink and walked across the street into the parking garage. I walked right over into the parking garage where they were and yelled at them for not sticking around to pay for the drink they ordered.

Things like this don't bother me, I suppose. Back in the Seventies when I was working for the Caterpillar Tractor Company in Illinois my best friend was Black. He had lots of friends on the south side of Chicago. One night, we drove to this fast food quick joint for a bite to eat. We got out of the car and walked up to the window. Y'know, plate glass window and metal slide underneath. He told me, "Whatever you do, don't leave my side," because he knew, being White, if I did, I'd be dead meat. He would often take me to meet his friends at their apartments. Of course, I was always the only White guy there. One time, we were all sitting in the living room of one of his friends. We heard two shots ring out right outside the door. My friend, familiar with this sound, immediately hit the floor. Me, not knowing what was going on, just sat there on the couch. A few moments later, someone in the room opened up the door and peeked outside. Two bodies lying on the ground. As I read in the paper the next day, one of the neighbors didn't like his neighbor's leaves blowing onto his lawn, so he shot them. I saw the police toss the bodies into the paddy wagon. So having to toss someone out of my coffee shop was chill with me. All I really cared about was how well I treated all my other customers and how well I made their drinks. One customer once told me, "Bill, you don't have to worry about that."

I should be making lots of espresso, being one of the best baristas in America, but instead I'm still going broke. One of life's injustices. The other day a rich couple came into the shop and both bought a small latte. In addition to making them each a small latte, I also made them happy. Imagine that. A poor man making a rich couple happy. Life goes on.

One day after work and I was doing my running up on Paseo de Vista, I got hit by a car. Not too badly tho, so I picked myself up with my left hand on his hood and my right hand on the pavement. I walked over to the driver of the car and saw that he was a customer, so I told him that I wanted to see him in my shop the next day. Saw him a week later with no hard feelings.

There was this woman staying at the La Fonda for a conference who wandered down to my shop for a coffee early in the morning. She intrigued me because of her exuberance, early in the morning. She lived in Michigan all her life, grew up in the country and now worked in the legal profession. She looked forward to retiring and moving to a warmer climate.

Maybe now is a good time to apologize to you for being a boring barista. Maybe you wanted me to tell you about Santa Fe and all of its galleries, parties, bars, wild times, rich gossip. Sorry, dude, I led a boring life here in Santa Fe. I wish I could tell you about all the incredible customers I served. Being a barista took so much out of me, pouring myself out for my customers, that at the end of the day I would collapse on the floor, cry, then clean up and go home to Helen.

One day a man asked me what's happening in Santa Fe, what's cool, where to go and what to do. I had to apologize to him and tell him that at the end of the day, I went home to Helen, we had a bite to eat, played a game of cribbage, watched a little TV, maybe read, and then we went to bed. I told him I led a quiet life. Two weeks later I received a T-shirt in the mail which said "Quiet Life." I still wear it every day on my morning walks during the summer.

If you're young and want job security without boredom but requires risk, become a barista, become the best, own a niche in a tourist town, and you will meet people from all over the world. Even tho you will be doing the same thing every day, no two days are alike. You will become a rock star.

But making excellent espresso was still tantamount in my life. The freshness of the espresso, the timing of the draw, the temperature and consistency of the milk, the presentation of the product: everything had to be perfect. Again I'll say this: how good is the drink and how well did I treat the customer consumed me. Which is why I believe I was the best barista in America. Against all odds, in New Mexico, I succeeded in being the best and longest running barista in Santa Fe. Again, not for the faint of heart.

Okay, more customers.

This guy is well known in Santa Fe. He was a cool customer. He would take Helen and me out for drinks and food. For instance, the third floor at the La Fonda, watching the sunset, on La Fonda's balcony. Or how about a small Chinese restaurant on Water Street, sitting outside. He paid for it all. He once got shot while standing in his driveway but did recover. It made the newspaper. He has apple trees, as well as other fruit trees, on his property. One of his apple trees was planted by Bishop Lamy a long, long time ago. Helen and I would pick his apples, take them home and apple press them, making apple juice. To this day, he lets us pick his apples. Nice guy.

The governor at the time promoted an out of state coffee corporation at the expense of local coffee shops, doing her part to put local coffee shops out of business. Bottom line: don't support a governor who disses local businesses.

Maybe now is a good time to let you know that while working my tiny coffee shop, I never got sick. I mean, the last time I got so sick so that I couldn't go to work was the Wednesday before Thanksgiving, 2005. And while I worked my tiny coffee shop, it was six days a week, 55 hours, year after year. Never missed a day and always opened up on time. Nobody else can claim that. Up until my last year, I opened up at six in the morning. Except for these three days.

On January 1st, I opened up at 5:55 am. Know anybody who opened up every January 1st at 5:55 am? I do because I thought it good and proper for the best barista in Santa Fe to be the first to make espresso every year. On Easter morning, I opened up at 5:55 am. On Christmas morning I opened up at 5:55 am. Christmas was my favorite day of the year to work. Everybody's happy. Little by little, I was beginning to get out of debt. Paid off all my credit cards and had a little left over to put in the bank.

Personal notes. When customers would come into my shop with worldly worries, I would tell them this sentence which began and ended with the same word: "Leave the world outside, it'll be there when you leave." People came into my shop to have a good time, get away from the outside, and I wasn't gonna let a bunch of customers ruin my day with a bunch of negativities. Not gonna happen. Maybe now is a good time to tell you that I lived by, and still do, a six word statement: Fun with all, sex with one. That one is Helen. The rest of you I get to have fun with. Here's another note: Being a dysfunctional Army brat, I operated under this mental umbrella: "It's my fault you're not pleased with me. What can I do to please you at my expense?" It's a miracle I survived as a business owner! I was a man of mistakes, but I did what it takes. I went through my days making people feel good so I could feel good myself. Easy to see why I wore myself out every day.

Went to a bar once on, of all days, Good Friday. Lo and behold, there was a good customer. Some days we would hang out at the Pink Adobe after work and sit outside drinking beers, watching Harley Davidsons go by. Once we had a beer at El Farol on Canyon Road. A bunch of weird looking locals having a good time. Don't think we ever went back.

Over the years different shops asked me to show them how to make espresso. On Canyon Road is The Tea House which, as the name implies, primarily sells teas. Then there's the woman who owns a coffee shop in the Design Center. Terrific woman. I told her there are absolutes which must be followed. Tamping pressure, amount of grounds, timing of the draw, temperature of the water, temperature of the milk. Procedure. Everything had to be done properly and in order. Each and every drink all the time, all the while conversing with the customer.

Damn it! What bothers me is the disrespect my profession gets in society. There are kids who don't know what they're doing, just pressing buttons and treating their job as if they're flipping burgers at McDonalds. They're dissing a respectable profession. Like handing your precious child off to a public school person who has never seen your child before and hoping for the best. Easy to see why we homeschooled Boaz, our one and only. Helen and I sacrificed being a one income family for the benefit of being a family. I guess I said all that to say this: If you can, find a dedicated barista to make your espresso.

The city of Grants, New Mexico, built a new coffee shop next to their new library and wanted me to run it for them. Helen and I stayed at the Sunset Motel on Route 66 for a weekend and it was like living in the past. Perfect. The city's PR person showed us around Grants and we got the royal treatment. Just up Route 66 is the town of Milan which has a diner which has, of all things, a big picture of a Cubs game on the wall that very few people have seen. Go to Milan, New Mexico on Route 66 if you want to see it. But after it was all over, we had to say no, since Helen and I were committed to Santa Fe.

Speaking of customers, let me tell you. Many of my customers were socially challenged and couldn't hold a decent conversation if their life depended on it. As much as I tried to converse with them and get them to open up, it was pretty much a one way conversation. This left me frustrated. Everybody wanted to know everything about me while they remained as tight as a clam, brought about by shame and guilt in their lives. What was I to do?

Then somehow, one day on YouTube, I saw this performer performing at the White House in front of Michelle and Barack Obama. A performer who has been around for years and you all know him. That's when I realized that I was meant to perform. I mean, performing gained me popularity in school growing up, always being the new kid on the block and not being popular. So instead of trying to engage in a meaningful conversation with my customer, I decided to perform for them. In other words, I dominated the conversation with fun and laughter. Wow! All of a sudden, serving coffee got a whole lot better. I wasn't expecting anything out of my customers and I was happy making them happy, along with making them an excellent drink. May I say, tips substantially increased. My customers were happy, I was happy; why didn't I think of this before?

If there was sadness in my job, it was standing outside in the morning, right after opening up at six in the morning. Yes, downtown Santa Fe is extremely beautiful in the morning, quiet and peaceful, watching Santa Fe wake up. I would wave to the cars as they drove by. Every now and then I would snag someone walking by and turn them into a customer. Of course they left a happy camper. But for the most part, I was lonely. Again, here I was with an excellent product and no one to serve it to.

Speaking of standing outside, here's an interesting note. Beginning in 1998, I noticed something interesting. Beginning in the middle of May to the middle of September, every day, a monarch butterfly would flutter by up San Francisco Street at about 11:30 in the morning. Year after year, right on schedule. During their busy season, so to speak, two would flutter by, the second one around 1:30 in the afternoon. I guess San Francisco Street was their flight pattern. I always enjoyed seeing them, year after year. And that's my secret.

One of my favorite customers was always smiling, perky plus and bubbly. Always a pleasure seeing her, always a pleasure serving her. One day she came in and told me she may have another spot for me if I wanted to place another cart there. In the Jean Cocteau Theater, now owned by George R. R. Martin. Didn't know how I could cut it but at least I was interested. So I said to pick me up at 3:30 after I finished cleaning up and we'll drive on over to take a look. She comes at three. Okay. We drive on over and here's the interesting part.

When I drive in downtown Santa Fe I am overly cautious and very conscientious, eyes darting to and fro, looking out for pedestrians (and there are a lot of pedestrians in downtown Santa Fe) and keeping my eyes wide open for that car that comes out of nowhere. She, on the other hand, is a happy-go-lucky driver, laughing and joking every block of the way. We are so different in our driving habits. This experience taught me to lighten up and enjoy my driving in downtown Santa Fe.

I did not accept the location but driving with her sure changed me. For the better.

Here's a somewhat funny story that I think you will enjoy. There was a small tech company a couple of blocks down the street from the shop and everyday about half a dozen of its employees would walk up to the shop for their coffee drink. But let me back up a little. A couple of months earlier, I would sprinkle bird seed in front of the shop on the street for the finches who lived in the parking garage across the street. It was entertaining to watch them eat. Then the neighborhood pigeons got in on the act and bullied the finches away. Whenever I saw this, I shooed the pigeons away. The pigeons didn't like this and I guess they vowed to get even. So they perched on the rooftop and whenever customers would come to the shop and sit outside, the pigeons would poop on my customers, on my umbrella and on my chairs. I was constantly cleaning up after them. Anyway, back to the tech company. Those pigeons would wait for this guy and his fellow employees to arrive and then poop on them. Unfortunately, there wasn't much I could do about it. Can't have them arrested. I asked my landlord to put up a plastic owl on the roof. He told me that wouldn't work because he had tried it before. So I stopped feeding the finches and eventually the pigeons stopped coming. Pigeons may be stupid but they're not dumb.

Another customer, over the years, owns a custom hat store in downtown Santa Fe. He was a customer from the Eldorado Hotel days. Always good to see him, always treated me with respect, and we enjoyed each other's company. I do miss him, along with his employee. I always called him Cowboy because he dressed like a cowboy. Rode a Harley.

Then there was the woman who manages a shop on the Plaza and would walk down just about every day for her latte. It was her pleasure to smoke a cigarette to and fro. She was a long time customer who went through a lot and would share with me her trials and tribulations. I would listen.

There was a couple who lived in Calgary, Alberta, Canada and would visit Santa Fe once a year. I loved this couple.

They were a little younger than me and they would always sit outside for a half hour, sipping their lattes. Just like the Europeans do. When I wasn't serving customers I would stand outside with them and we would talk. Rarely, and I mean rarely, would I ever sit with a customer outside. Just the way I am, I guess. I always stood. One time they asked me if I had a choice of restaurants to eat at and I told them: If I had one last meal before the firing squad, it would be Bouche. Just a couple of blocks away, within walking distance. It's now Mille. The menu, expensive of course, is French country and is strictly farm to table. They gave Helen and me a gift certificate to eat at Bouche. May I say, it was the best meal Helen and I ever had. First time we ever had foie gras. I miss them very much because of their friendliness.

Helen and our vacations were simple: Helen and Boaz and I would drive to California in September right after Labor Day when summer was officially over and Santa Fe became a ghost town. Then in November, after Boaz joined the Army, Helen and I would drive to Florida for my mama's birthday. Mama's now a hundred years old. She lives in the Villages but I would get away to visit my brother in Merritt Island, shop a little at Ron Jon's surf shop, and go boogie boarding in the ocean. While staying at my brother's house I got bit by a spider while sleeping. That resulted in a six week discomfort. While boogie boarding in the ocean I got bit by a shark. That meant dripping blood through the lobby on my way to see my brother on the pier.

In California, we house sat for a retired couple in San Clemente. I will never forget the first time we visited San Clemente. I'm telling you the truth: it blew me away. I ain't never seen anything like it. We picked up some picnic items at the local Safeway and had our picnic on the beach, just south of the pier. This was an OMG moment. Why didn't anyone tell me just how cool this place was. This was so cool! Metro link in back of us, the ocean in front of us, we're drinking wine, eating cheese, crackers and fruit, enjoying some of the best California has to offer. All the while sitting on the beach. To this day, San Clemente is my favorite beach. I like its waves. Before we drove back to Santa Fe, Boaz and I bought a couple of boogie boards. Next year, we boarded in the water for some good father son water time. Helen would walk the beach.

Alas, all good things do come to an end. The couple we house sat for moved to Redding. This meant, we're now staying with Helen's cousins in San Diego. We're grateful to them for putting us up. Boaz and I would sleep out on the porch while Helen slept inside. We went swimming in the community pool. One night we went out to eat at this fancy restaurant on the beach. Such an oo-la-la time. Helen's cousin paid for it all. Actually, I tipped the car getter, which was funny. Helen's cousin is a manager at a factory which makes missile and satellite parts. Plays acoustical guitar at home in his off times.

One year Helen stayed with her sister in Phoenix while Boaz and I drove to Alamo Lake State Park in Arizona. It was good father son time all by ourselves. I let Boaz drive part way to fulfill his drivers ed requirements. On another occasion, Boaz and I camped at a beach park in California. Had another great time. That's when I walked into our tent and saw a black widow crawling up to my pillow. Needless to say, she didn't live long. Then I walked outside and saw another spider on my wetsuit. Time to kill another spider.

The next year we stayed at Helen's other cousin. Both of Helen's cousins are quite well to do. I guess ya gotta be to live in San Diego. All four of us went out to eat at Croce's Restaurant and Jazz Bar, owned by Jim's widow. I understand she was instrumental in revitalizing downtown San Diego. Helen's cousin owned a T-Bird convertible and he and Boaz would cruise San Diego, all the while being the tour guide. San Clemente's beach is an hour's drive from San Diego so I decided to boogie board down at Dog Beach. A little closer. That's when Helen and I discovered Hodads Bar and Grill. A lot of license plates on the walls. Anyway, I wanted to graduate from boogie board to a surf board. There was a surf shop about a mile up the street from the Dog Beach and I drove up and bought myself a surfboard and a wetsuit. I was ready to go.

Drove back to Dog Beach and tried my luck at surfing. This did not go well. When I landed on the beach, the lifeguard came up to me and said. "Are you all right?" I told him, yeah, I'm all right. It's just that I live in New Mexico and don't get to the ocean very often.

Back when Boaz graduated from home school we held a living room graduation ceremony, calling our home school El Rancho Road Academy. It's all videotaped. As I said, Boaz enlisted into the Army which left only Helen and I driving to San Diego. Boaz is now a Green Beret in Special Forces and has been deployed five times in the Middle East. I mention this because we both go the distance. It's in our DNA. Which is why, when you get to the end of this book, you will see that I went the distance.

Anyway, the next day I drove up to San Clemente to try my luck at surfing on the north side of the pier. This did not go well. After twenty-two tries, I'm walking up the beach when I notice a man with a long surfboard. He has surfed all over the world. He said, "Bill, you got the wrong surfboard. What you need to do is drive up to Costco at Dana Point and buy one of their ninety-nine dollar surfboards. That will be more to your liking." So I drove up to Costco, walked in, wet, in my wetsuit and said, I'm not a member but I'd like to become a member so I can buy one of your surfboards. To this day, you will see me on the back of my Costco card wearing my wetsuit. I eventually went back to that surf shop, dropped off the surfboard they sold me and I gave the owner my card and said, send me a check for whatever you deem right. A couple of weeks later I got a check in the mail. Still got the wet suit tho.

Back at San Clemente, I tried surfing again. Didn't work. That's when I realized, I don't want to be on top of the water, I would rather be in the water, like on a boogie board. I eventually sold that surfboard for twenty dollars at a surf shop. I'm here to tell you, boogie boards are easier to fit into a Honda than a surfboard.

It's now November and it's time to drive down to Florida. Well, the day before we were to leave, I walked into the shop and I could smell death in the air. My La Marzocco had given up the ghost. Time to put the sign out and head down south. Helen and I, while in Florida, visited Disney World, my favorite place on earth. That's when I ordered a new espresso machine, this time a Synesso. They're made in Seattle don't you know. It was hooked up the day we got back to Santa Fe and, as far as machines go, the best purchase I ever made. That machine never gave me a lick of trouble.

Back to California. One time after boogie boarding and Helen was thrift store shopping, I was waiting to be picked up, thinking, I sure could use a beer from the store across the street where I would always buy a beer after playing in the ocean. But I had no money. Bummer, dude. All of a sudden, this lady with a van full of coolers drives up, needing all of her coolers taken down to the beach, no small feat considering all the stairs she was gonna have to manipulate So I told her, Lady, I'm waiting for Helen to pick me up but if you loan me five dollars for a couple of beers, I will take all your coolers down for you and pay you back when Helen arrives. She gives me a ten, I take all her coolers down the steps for her, I buy myself a couple of beers while waiting for Helen, I give the lady her money back and I am one happy camper.

One customer who lived in San Diego was a very high end hair dresser who had clients in Santa Fe. He would fly to Santa Fe just a few times a year to do their hair. He owned a sailboat which he kept on Mission Bay in San Diego. He would take us sailing and it was fun being out on the water. But that's when I realized that I would rather be in the water instead of on the water. I think we went sailing three times but it sure was pleasant because he was such a good host.

There is a man named on San Francisco Street who owns a genuine local restaurant and has been on San Francisco Street for about forty years now. He took it over from his parents. He would come by in the morning before he opened up and get himself a coffee. What a terrific friend. Low key, easy going, always thinking of his restaurant. When customers would come into my shop asking for a place to eat breakfast, I would always direct them to his restaurant which was practically across the street. It was, and still is, genuine Santa Fe. One year when the Soccer World Cup was being played, his employees had a TV in the kitchen, watching every game. When it came time for the United States to play, I closed up shop and, with his permission, watched the game in the kitchen of his restaurant. Again, genuine Santa Fe.

When I first started working at the shop, I found free parking over by the skateboard park just three blocks away. One morning while pulling up to park for the day, a street sweeper backs into my car and crunches the front end. I eventually get the City to pay for it. Then one day, on a Wednesday before Thanksgiving, I found my car stolen. I called the police and they informed me that my car was towed and is now impounded. So now I'm without a car for the entire Thanksgiving weekend. I called my friend at the City and he told me who to talk to. I called this man on Monday and he agreed with me that it was wrong for my car to have been towed on the day before Thanksgiving. He informed me that the reason my car was towed was because I had the wrong license plate. More on that later. Eventually I was able to get free parking in the lot next to my shop.

So now I'm standing in front of the judge, again, and when she asked me how I pleaded, I shouted out, "Not Guilty!" I told her it was because the license plate on file is not my license plate. She gets on her laptop and says to me, "You're right. That license plate belongs to someone who lives on my block." Case dismissed. That's when I go into my dismissal dance because all bets are off. Oh yeah.

Speaking of license plates, one of the pleasures I got from working across the street from the parking garage was seeing all the different license plates from across the country drive into the parking garage. The most popular out of state plates were, in this order, Texas, California, Colorado, Arizona, and, for some strange reason, Michigan was number five. Florida wasn't far behind. I enjoyed looking at all the different tourist cars coming into Santa Fe. Especially during the summer. Crazy looking vehicles driving up San Francisco Street going toward the Plaza. Apparently, Santa Fe was on a lot of people's bucket list. Strange looking campers, RVs, bumper stickered vans, packed out Harleys, you name it. Lots of Harleys over the Memorial Day weekend, spillovers from the motorcycle rally held up in Angel Fire.

Wanna know what locals like to do? Hop in the car, sometimes with the family, and drive to the Plaza. This is their Plaza and they were gonna make full use of it. This was the highlight of their day. Well, one day, a petition went around downtown Santa Fe to block off San Francisco Street for pedestrians only. You know, the way they do in Europe. The Santa New Mexican newspaper got wind of this and wrote an article about it. I can tell you, the locals were not gonna have any of this. So for the next three days after the article was written, it was bumper to bumper traffic on San Francisco Street up to the Plaza in protest to wanting San Francisco Street blocked off for pedestrians only. You can get away with blocking streets off in Europe, but not in Santa Fe. Needless to say, the street was never blocked. But it sure was fun seeing all the cars go by for three straight days. A lot of cars had protest signs on them and a lot of cars were waving the American flag. Bottom line? Don't mess with Santa Fe.

At this point in time, I enjoyed being the best. Oh how I loved my customers. And they knew it. Every day customers would take pictures of me and videotape my shop. You should have been there. One week, National Geographic was holding a convention at the Eldorado Hotel. One of their photographers came in and took several pictures of me. Two months later, I received in the mail a wonderful 11x14 canvassed picture of me. National Geographic made me look good. The picture is in my office. It's the picture on the back of this book.

Oh! I guess I should tell you about the six walls on my property. All being built while I worked the espresso cart. The first wall was a retaining wall on the south side of the house. An embankment was created by the leveling of the slope for the house and needed to be shored up to prevent erosion. It's over 100 feet long and rises above six feet. Oh my back! That's when I realized: Egypt may have built the pyramids but China built the Great Wall. Then I thought of all the sore backs that went before mine. I felt one with history.

The next wall was the one around the vegetable garden. Only about a couple of feet tall, its perimeter is about 150 feet. The next wall is around our other garden. It's about one to two feet tall and its perimeter is about 90 feet. The fourth wall is another retaining wall and it averages about two feet tall and 50 feet in length, on the north side of the house. The fifth wall is only about a foot tall, around the flower garden, and it's about 80 feet in length.

Now for the last wall. Another retaining wall. My friend had gouged out the side of the hill when he finished creating our driveway. I asked him and he delivered a bunch of broken sidewalk and dropped everything along the side of the hill which he created when he carved out our driveway. Time to put that broken sidewalk and a lot stones to work. This was probably around 2015. Every day Helen would relieve me from work at 12:30 and I would go home and do a bag of mortar. I had about two hours to do a bag. This gave me about one foot by ten foot of accomplishment. Then I'd go back to work and close up. Mortar and coffee, that was my life. This took several months to accomplish. When it was all finished, I created a 120 foot wall, beginning at one foot, rising to five feet, then sloping back down to one foot. At last, I was finished! Six walls on our property.

In March of 2020 when Covid struck, lots of shops and restaurants were closing. Well, I could have stayed open since I was under the radar, but for good PR, I closed up for a month. The only reason was because I had a month's worth of projects that needed to be done at home and on the property. I kept a journal of everything I did. Four pages worth. At the end of one month all my projects were completed so I went back to work.

Did I tell you? After we moved into our home, we planted trees: fifty oak trees, fifty buffalo bushes (all lining our two hundred foot driveway), fifteen elm trees and half a dozen fruit trees. Planting trees in Santa Fe is no easy task. The soil is hard and rocky and everything you plant needs to be watered. On a drip system. We have hundreds of feet of dripline which we bought from Firebird.

One more thing. I guttered our house and garage and bought a fifteen hundred gallon tank with the five hundred dollar tip Helen received on Mother's Day while working the cart at the Eldorado Hotel. We bought the water tank from Firebird and now all the runoff water from our garage and house collects into that tank.

Now I could fully focus on the shop. I opened up at six in the morning, as usual, and quickly drove to Albertson's for milk. Now I was ready. Getting a bit older now and I needed to change my hours. So I opened up at seven in the morning and closed at three in the afternoon. I was settling into my routine. Go to Albertson's at six, get to the shop, set up, then open up at seven, six days a week. But alas, my body was beginning to wear down. I mean, c'mon, fifteen years, six days a week, 55 hours, never missing a day, not being late, there's only so much a body can do, as much as I love my job. So eventually, I lessened my hours to four days a week, 28 hours. Still, at the end of each day, I would just collapse on the floor until I got up to clean up. I poured myself out for my customers. I could have slept in the back of a sinking boat.

There's something I should tell you. Across from Albertson's where I would buy my milk is Rosario Cemetery. At six o'clock in the morning, when I would be getting my milk, that cemetery would be packed with hundreds of cars, parked bumper to bumper, with overflow parking in the Albertson's parking lot. Six o'clock in the morning! Once, the next morning, the same thing. Santa Fe is family.

Did I tell you about a docent at the Georgia O'Keeffe Museum. The Georgia O'Keeffe Museum is behind the Eldorado Hotel on Johnson Street and this docent would stop by almost every day. The Georgia O'Keeffe Museum opened up when I was serving espresso at the Eldorado Hotel. This was a big event. Anyway, we became good friends. He had the responsibility of overseeing Georgia O'Keeffe's exhibitions worldwide. That meant videotaping the packing up of the paintings, driving to the airport with the boxed paintings, videotaping the boxed paintings being placed on the plane, traveling on the plane with the paintings, then videotaping the paintings off the plane, and transporting the paintings to the museum, making sure the paintings were properly hung. The museum had the responsibility of the security. Quite the responsibility. Whenever Georgia's works went abroad, let's say, London, Vienna, Paris, wherever, he was in charge. And whenever Georgia's pictures went on tour, it was three cities per tour.

Here's a particular tour. A Georgia tour would last nine months, three months in each city. One tour involved London. London has always had an infatuation with America's Wild West. You know, Bill Cody, Wild Bill Hickock, Annie Oakley, that sort of thing. The exhibition in London attracted over one million visitors with lines out the door.

One time, when Georgia's pictures were transported from the delivery truck to the museum, two guys were carrying two of her pictures. One of the two pictures dropped. My friend the docent scolded them and said, "One picture at a time." The reason I'm mentioning this is because, being a barista and doing two things at a time while making the espresso drink and conversing with the customer, I came to multitask. Then my docent friend told me seven words that changed my life: "One at a time, make two trips." Thanks to him, my retirement years are a bit more enjoyable.

He liked Helen and I so much that he showed us Georgia O'Keeffe's secret basement belongings. Her paint brushes, her tubes of paint, her secret paintings, everything Georgia left behind and carefully preserved. He showed us what very few people have seen. The security system is so high tech that, when activated, a one degree temperature change in the room will inform security immediately.

The famous photographer Annie Leibovitz once visited the Georgia O'Keeffe Museum. My docent friend was kind enough to walk her over to my shop a couple of times. Let me tell you, she is so nice. It was easy to engage in a conversation with her. It was interesting standing in front of the photographer whose pictures of all my favorite rock stars I had long admired.

We owned a Honda Element, the first green one in Santa Fe actually, and used it to transport our catering cart around. This nice man from New York City held his wedding reception at the Georgia O'Keeffe Museum and we catered it. Took two trips to transport everything over to the museum and everything worked out swell. This man came into the shop the day after and reiterated what a joy it was to have us coffee cater his wedding reception. Yes, I had to make two ramps in order to place the catering cart into the Honda Element, but that's what it takes to make a business work.

Did I tell you about Mario? A most interesting individual. Nothing special about him really but he's consistent and genuine Santa Fe. When he first showed up at my cart at the Eldorado Hotel, thought he was a bit out of it, if you know what I mean. Come to be, Mario was one of my favorite customers. For over twenty years, Mario was usually one of my first customers in the morning. Mario worked for the city and his responsibility was keeping every parking meter in the city working. Mario would tell me about the stupid things people did to the meters and how he had to replace them. You know, shoving counterfeit coins into the meter and jamming them up. Once there was a movie being made on Washington Street and Mario had to remove, at the request of the movie producer, all the meters for the filming. Or the time a movie had a chase scene in the parking garage across the street in the middle of the night and Mario had the responsibility of removing all the cars.

While at the Eldorado Hotel, one of my favorite customers was a hotel employee. We would go out drinking and hang out on balconies. Then we would hold hands and go skipping down San Francisco Street, merrily, merrily, down the street, laughing all the way. He and I always had a good time. Don't know whatever happened to him though. I suppose friends come and go.

Sad time now. In June of 2012, I found out my dad was dying. I took it hard. Incredible life he led. Married seventy years, eight kids, umpteen years in the Army, World War II and the Korean Conflict (which is why we moved every three and a half years), manager of the employment office in Illinois' second largest city, went on to become a deacon in the Catholic Church and eventually, at the advice of his doctor, moved to Florida. Later that year when I found out daddy was dying, I took off work and drove down to see him. I held his hand while he was lying in bed and all the typical father son difficulties melted away. Daddy died in January 2013 a week after his ninety-third birthday. As a tradition, all of us kids called him up on his birthday, told him we loved him, and what a good father he was. A week later, daddy checked out in his sleep, a happy camper. Because I had to get back to work, I couldn't stick around for his twenty-one gun salute at the National Cemetery in Leesburg, Florida. The officer in charge of the ceremony said he never saw a more decorated soldier. It was during these days that I did not treat my customers very well. I was hurt, I was angry, and I took it out on my customers. Well, life goes on.

At this time, I devoted myself to becoming the best barista in America. The best latte, the best coffee shop, the best coffee. Oh, how many times did I hear: this is the best coffee I ever had or this is the best espresso I've had since coming to America, the best everything. Even my little fifty two square foot coffee shop was looking good. Remember that one fluorescent light fixture I had in the ceiling? Well, I asked if I could have two more light fixtures. So I called up the owner of the company that made the light fixture panels and bought two more really cool light fixture panels. At last, I'm running on all eight cylinders.

The walls were covered, lots of pictures, perfect paint... easy to see why, every day, people would take video of me and my shop. Okay, I'll say it again: you should have been there.

About the Cubs and the World Series. When I knew they would be in it, I rented a rental car, made Helen run the shop and drove to Chicago. Actually, I stayed with my sister in Rockford and figured out the train system to Wrigley Field. I watched the games at the John Barleycorn Bar in Wrigleyville. For me, this was way cool. Inside the bar, watching the games, the TVs were muted during the commercials and songs were played. Everyone in the bar knew the lyrics and everyone sang along to every song. I was in Wrigleyville for four games. When the final game was won, everyone in the bar erupted in excitement and threw their beers into the air. The place was drenched. We all left the bar wet with beer and everyone was crowded outside. I eventually made my way, along with the crowd, back to the train. This time I stayed with my graphics designer and slept on the floor. In the morning after, I drove back to Santa Fe.

Here's an interesting story I think you'll like. As mentioned, my dad was in the Army and we moved every three and a half years. Home base was Aurora, Illinois. Whether we lived in Corning, Iowa, Fort Benning, Georgia, Munich, Germany, or Park Forest, Illinois, we always visited Aurora, where Grandma and Grandpa lived. I would take him fishing later on. Anyway, there was a rock half buried on the corner of their house that us kids would step on while playing outside. I am mentioning this because in the midst of constantly moving round, whenever we visited Grandma and Grandpa's house, there was that rock, half buried in the ground on the corner of their house. That rock was a constant as we constantly moved around. And while working the shop in Santa Fe, I would occasionally visit Aurora, and there, while standing outside on the sidewalk, next to the green Honda Element, I would wish I could have that rock, now that Grandma and Grandpa were dead.

While in Illinois for the World Series, I visited Aurora and parked outside Grandma and Grandpa's house, standing on the sidewalk, again, wishing I had that rock. Then I saw three Hispanic guys working on the property. I think they now owned the house. So I walked up to them as they were working and said to them, "I'm looking for a rock that's been on this property for years and years." They looked at me as if I was crazy. I finally found that rock, still there, underneath a pile of wood, still half buried in the ground. I asked them, "May I have that rock?" They looked at me and said, "You want that rock?" Yes! I asked them to get me a shovel, I dig up the rock, hook up a hose in the basement of the bakery to wash the rock, and with the help of these three Hispanics, roll the rock into the back seat of the rental car. I'm making an incredibly long story short here. Talk to me if you want the full story. So I'm down in the basement of the pastry shop us kids would frequent back in the 1950s, hooking up the hose. Back then, the bakery had a soda pop machine and it was the first time I ever had a Nehi strawberry soda. Golly it was good. How strange to be in the bakery's basement fifty years hence. The Nehi strawberry soda turned my lips red. Loved it! Anyway, I seat belted the rock in the back seat of the rental car. The head honcho who helped me said, "Good thing you got this rock today because next week we're gonna lay cement for a driveway and that rock was gonna have to be removed." After the Cubs won the World Series, I drove that rock back home. The rock that was a constant in my "here and there life" now sits on our property.

But wait, there's more! After the atomic bomb was invented in Los Alamos, the secrets were given to the Russians in Santa Fe at, allegedly, four different locations. One of those locations, allegedly, was at the Defouri Bridge. Lo and behold, the bridge became so dilapidated that, I believe in 2016, it had to be demolished and replaced. While it was in the process of its restoration, I stopped my car and parked it over at Alpine Lumber, walked on over to the now demolished bridge, and I ask the man, again Hispanic, "Please sir, may I have that rock down there?" He says, as those three guys before, "You want that rock?" which was lying in the bottom of the Santa Fe River, the United States' designated most endangered river. "Yes, may I have it?" So he walks down into the dry riverbed, retrieves the rock, and hands it off to me. I thanked him and walked back to my car at Alpine Lumber and drove it home. So, I said all that to say this: on our property is a rock which had been in the family for generations and a rock which belonged to a bridge which played a part in our world's history. Both rocks are placed next to a sign which belonged to the Very Large Array, down near Magdalena, New Mexico.

Did I tell you about that? While Helen and I visited the Very Large Array, as we were leaving from the gift shop I saw this sign in a ditch that had been run over a long time ago. I know it was a long time ago because where it was bent was now rusted out and Magdalena doesn't get much rain. So I took that sign, put it in the Honda Element, drove it home where it now sits on our property next to the two rocks.

Shortly thereafter, my nephew, who lived in Rockford, died. So I decided to close up shop and drive up to his funeral. A couple of mentions: Driving Highway 56 in the middle of the night through New Mexico, Oklahoma, and into Kansas, is a very lonely stretch of road. You can go for an hour without seeing another car. And very dark; sorta scary being all alone. Made it to Rockford, met lots of relatives, and saw the line out the door for three hours to pay respects to my sister, in the community hall for such occasions. My nephew was popular.

Here's a good story. That night it snowed. Driving out of Rockford early the next morning, about the only vehicles out at this time of day under such conditions were individual pick-up trucks with a snow plow attached. And me. Needed air in my tire, which I filled in Davenport, Iowa, on a Sunday morning. The gas station had a tiny store, where I bought a drink. The atmosphere was so heavenly in that store that I lingered a while, just to take it all in. Back on the road, I-80, I was looking for a particular store. Google directed me to Williamsburg. Found the store, not exactly what I was looking for, across the street from a church, so I headed out of town. I was driving through the neighborhood on the way out of town, and what did I see. A small town, middle America, early on Sunday morn, covered in snow. The streets were already plowed. The sidewalks and the steps and the side walls leading down from the house to the sidewalk were all covered with snow. Very quiet, very peaceful, very beautiful. It looked like a Norman Rockwell painting. Just a little bit of heaven on earth. Now, out of town, I'm back on I-80, which is about three miles from Williamsburg, and I'm headed west, going back home, this time sticking to the interstate. No more two lane highways for me.

Back to work. Oftentimes, during the winter, 6:30 am, opening up was a bit difficult. My supplies were kept in the back of the building where the shop was and I would walk back to the space there. Same place where I cleaned my utensils and airpots at the end of the day. Oh, that bitter morning cold wind from the north would sting my body and my face and my hands. But I knew I had to keep on keeping on. Even when the temperature was below freezing and the wind made it feel like the North Pole. Eighteen below zero one day? Yep! And I opened up on time, ready to rock and roll. One of the secrets to business longevity is daily consistency. Even when my tiny fifty square foot hole in the wall had no HVAC system. During the winter I heated the place up with two heaters and during the summer I cooled the shop down with two fans. That's it. I'm telling ya, it takes determination and persistence to make this place work.

One morning when Helen drove me to work (remember, we're a one car family) a car had driven into the parking lot wall and the car horn was blaring away. Two parking garage employees were already there, scoping out the situation, so I didn't get involved. Eventually the police arrived and disabled the honking horn. At this time, the driver of the car was crying his eyes out while a white sheet was placed over the passenger. You know what that means. Eventually, the car was towed away. An interesting way to start the day, wouldn't you say?

But the joy I experienced in the morning, standing outside the shop, waving to the vehicles as they drove by, is something very few people will ever experience in Santa Fe. The only pain, other than the cold wind during the winter, was watching cups from up the street go by. If they only knew how much better I was than what they were about to drink. But hey, let's stay positive. When a customer did walk in, I was salivating like Pavlov's dog. Sometimes I would get so excited that I would say something I shouldn't have said. I'd like to say we learn from our mistakes but I don't think I ever did. Except on my last day. I bit my tongue and remained silent. To this day, I'm glad I did. Y'know, silence is golden.

One gentleman I served was one of the three producers of Woodstock. He also produced concerts for every major rock group in America during the seventies and eighties. He's retired now but every year in Santa Fe he would put on the Antiquities Show. One year, while catering the show, for some reason, I started throwing up blood. My doctor immediately said, "Get yourself to the hospital!" Having only one car, (having only one car can make for a successful marriage because you have to communicate with your spouse to get the wheels and, in America, mobility is God) I drove to the Antiquities Show so Helen could drive me to the hospital, where I stayed for two days while Helen had to run the catering cart all by herself. What a way to make a living. Christus Hospital treated me like the customer of a five star hotel.

We no longer, after eighteen years, do catering. We sold the catering cart to the owner of Henry and the Fish. So comes to an end our catering. A final closure on a lot of work, but it was fun. Got to meet lots of people.

Let's do a quick go-back to the mall days. A man in black, dressed up like the pastor Robin Bullock, who walked back and forth every day for a week. Or the teenage shooting which took place just a hundred feet from our cart. I think the bullet hole is still in the ceiling. And the manager of the mall, who got fired one day, just like that. How mysterious, and nobody knew why.

There was a time when being a barista I hated my job and I hated my life. Those days are now gone. Yes I get depressed when business is slow but my oh my, I'm having the career of my life now, enjoying my job and now making those I serve happy. I'm telling you, when a customer comes in I'm thinking, oh yeah! Another person I can make happy. I'm satisfied because I can perform and deliver. Sell well and live!

Here's more about some customers now, saving the best for last. But first: There was a "starving artist" who did excellent work. She penciled a picture of the front of my coffee shop which now hangs inside of the shop and has been quite admired by my customers. Eventually she had to move home to her parents in Chicago. She attended a Boston Marathon, babysitting her two nieces while her sister ran the marathon. Then it happened. While holding the hands of her two nieces, waiting for her sister to come running by, the two bombs exploded and she was caught in between with her two nieces. What to do? She, along with her two nieces, eventually made it to safety. Why am I telling you this? When she got back home to her parents in Chicago, she wrote an extremely detailed account of what she went through with her nieces, the mayhem that ensued, the people running to and fro, the confusion she was engulfed in, her emotions and her eventual escape to safety. It's all written down on seven 11x13 pieces of parchment paper which are scrolled up and now sitting in my office at home. I don't think anyone else has seven sheets of parchment paper in their possession, detailing the account of the Boston Marathon bombing. Makes for an interesting read.

Then there's an early morning customer, Sparky, who worked at the Los Alamos National Laboratory. She was always late for work but still managed to keep her job.

Then there's a drug dealer who eventually got caught and

put on probation. Not allowed to leave the state and having to give urine tests every month, he sold expensive cars at a car dealer in Santa Fe to kill the time. He is a character and we thoroughly enjoyed each other. He went so far as to make postcards for me. His money, which he made while drug dealing, is in an undisclosed location. After probation, he moved to California with his girlfriend. He now lives somewhere else but we still keep in touch.

Then, like out of the blue, this violin player shows up, excellent in his profession: played at the Opera, Lensic, around the world, private gatherings, a good friend. To this day, Helen and I have his birdbath in front of our house, which he gave us. On permanent loan, I guess. I fill it every morning, unless I'm too tired to do so. Helen and I will, for as long as we own this property, take care of his birdbath.

Another violin player was a beautiful young Jewish woman who was a busker and would often play her violin on Burro Alley with her dog lying by her side. Sometimes after work I would walk up to Burro Alley and listen to her play. When Passover rolled around, I would wish her a meaningful Passover and she would tell me that she was having a Seder with some of her friends. When Hanukkah rolled around, I would wish her a happy Hanukkah. Hanukkah is important. I have two of her CDs.

Then there's this quantum physicist who taught physics at Santa Fe High School. When we were teaching Boaz algebra, we put an algebra problem on the whiteboard and for a full week, we all tried to figure out the answer. Couldn't do it. So I wrote the problem down on a sheet of paper and took it to my physicist friend. Of course he figured out the answer in twenty seconds. One day I was conversing with a customer who told me he lived in Montclair, New Jersey. I said, "Oh, I know someone who lives in Montclair." He exclaims, "I know him! We drink coffee together. He's that crazy Israeli who uses the F word in every other sentence." I said, "Yep, that's him." Small world.

And now for my most favorite customer, of all the

customers I had. She was the best, so here goes. Can't exactly remember when she first came into the shop but we agreed upon drinking a growler of beer in back of the espresso cart after work. So there we were, sitting behind the cart on a couple of crates, drinking beer from the growler, which I picked up from the Second Street Brewery at the railyard station. Well, we started drinking. We can't exactly remember everything but we pretty much trashed the back of the shop. The Raven map on the back wall was shredded (had to buy a new one), blood was all over her face, which I needed to clean off, there was so much blood on my shirt that when I got home, Helen said the shirt we'll throw away but your jeans I'll wash. Can't remember what excuse I gave Helen but I guess it worked. What a wild time we had.

To this day, her spattered blood is still on the back wall of the shop, Well, when it came time for her to leave the shop after our wild time together, she rode her bicycle away. I knew something was wrong when, before going a hundred feet, two cars honked at her. Come to find out two days later that she had crashed her bike, somehow got taken to Christus St. Vincent Hospital, bruised up, and in the middle of the night, woke up with an IV in her arm and her bicycle next to her bed. So she pulls the IV out of her arm, gets on her bicycle and rides out of the hospital to home. Wherever that is at this point in time. She shows up at my shop two days later, bruised, and explains the situation.

But here is what's interesting about her and why I was so infatuated with her. Okay, she lived out of the back of her pickup truck. She's homeless. Either showered outside where she stayed every now and again or showered in a local gym which gave her privilege. She used to live in New York City and rode her bicycle around for fifteen years. Played chess in Washington Park with the old guys, always beating them. One day, while she was in my shop, we turned on an Albuquerque radio station. She knew all the lyrics to all the songs played and sang them out loud. Even when a Spanish song came on, she explicitly sang those lyrics in Spanish as well. But wait, there's more! When a Michael Jackson song came on, she did the moon walk in front of my cart, better than Michael Jackson could have done.

I always gave her coffee. Oft times I would keep a beer in my fridge so when she came to the shop, I'd put a beer in a cup and she would sit outside with her beer, which looked like a latte.

One day, I turned the radio up so we could hear it outside. Golly, we danced up a storm. So much so that the cars which drove by honked their horns and shouted in approval with their windows rolled down. We were quite the couple, dancing in front of the shop. Being somewhat homeless, she texted me and asked if she could spend the night at our house. I told her no. This is another regret I will have to live with for the rest of my life. And no, we never kissed.

Alas, all good things do come to an end (except for my marriage, which seems to go on forever) so I'll explain the rest in the epilogue.

On my way home from work one day, I received another parking ticket for running a stop sign. Time to stand in front of a judge. Again. The judge couldn't read the parking ticket so the case was dismissed. Dismissal dance time again. In the twenty-eight years I spent in Santa Fe, I think this made the fifth time I had to stand in front of a judge. Wild child indeed.

Over the years, I noticed a peculiar change in my customers. Let me explain. First of all, now with the baby boomers booming into retirement at the rate of 10,000 a day, I'm seeing an influx of retired couples doing a two night stand. Oh how often I heard the question, "So we got two days in Santa Fe, what's there to do and what should we see?" So I told them the usual jive: Plaza, galleries, churches, hiking trails, restaurants, the Federal Courthouse where Billy the Kid was arraigned, but mostly, just put your walking shoes on and walk around. One time when I was walking around the Plaza, it started to rain so we all huddled underneath a portal. I overheard six different languages and not one of them was English. Indeed, Santa Fe attracts people from all over the world.

Then there were young couples, Millennials I guess, who would walk up to the shop, see my sign outside the shop, do their research on their phones, read the reviews and walk on in. And before they left, I would hear them say "The reviews were right: he really is the best."

I was beginning to get tired so I decided to sell the shop. I sold it to a guy whose name I won't mention. He owned the shop for nine months but I made the mistake of not getting the money up front. After nine months, he reneged on the contract and filed for bankruptcy. Oh well. At least I was able to build three more rock walls on our property. But after six rock walls, I told Helen, I'm getting too old for this. Time to go back to work.

Now begins the last three years of my making espresso. Undoubtedly the best three years of all.

Everyone was glad to see me back because the guy ran the shop into the ground. It was fun to be back at work. Ordering coffee, making espresso, picking up milk on a daily basis early in the morning at Albertson's, ice from the Hilton, making sure I had the right amount of supplies, that sort of thing. My last three years at being a barista in Santa Fe were cool. The product and the customers were great. Silly note: for pastries, we bought cinnamon dots at Sam's Club and sold them for fifty cents apiece. In a small shop, sell small pastries. In a box I made at the Eldorado Hotel. I had a ten foot 1x4 piece of wood and the hotel let me use their workshop in the basement. Used every inch of that wood. That box still sits on the counter in the shop. The shop that's still not being used. Anyway, in a nutshell, I was finally happy.

More about my customers.

Two young women from Texas, dressed to the nines wearing high class Neiman Marcus wear, smelling mighty fine, along with their sugar daddy who was ruggedly handsome to boot. During Covid when I was open, a man, who didn't buy any coffee, for a couple of months would come in, slam a twenty dollar bill on the counter, say "Thanks for being open," then walk away. Or what about this man who comes in, asks me how I'm doing. So I tell him: "I'm Captain Fantastic, Jumpin' Jack Flash and Luke Skywalker all rolled up in one." He tips me a hundred dollar bill and, with his Americano in his hand, I ask him, "Who are you?" He responds, "Just a man" and walks away. Lately I was getting five dollar tips. Lots of them. People seemed to like me. My customers would tell me that if I left, there goes the business. Sorta like, take Mick Jagger out of the picture and there go the Rolling Stones.

Some of my customers were retired. Like a couple who drove around on an orange Harley Davidson that they named Clementine. Another retired couple lived in Beverly Hills, California and visited once a year. They were long time customers from the Eldorado Hotel days. There was a customer who was so bodacious that he could get away with parking backwards in front of the shop while the parking police were standing across the street and he never got a ticket. There was a sweet young couple still trying to find their place in life who would come in everyday. Then they moved on. A woman who worked for the Lensic and would come in every day. We talked baseball, she Boston Red Sox and me Chicago Cubs.

Summers were good because I served a lot of tourists. They would sit out front on the chairs and enjoy themselves. Underneath the umbrella. As mentioned, many were two night standers whom I wouldn't see anymore because they were just passing through and Santa Fe was on their bucket list. I would also get those from the Albuquerque Balloon Fiesta in October in the afternoon after the morning ascension.

The Lensic Theater would hold afternoon concerts and the musicians would stop in before their rehearsals. I enjoyed getting to know them over the years. They all looked so good dressed in black when they came into the shop. On a side note, the manager of the Lensic at the time was kind enough to give Helen and I comps whenever there was an evening performance that we wanted to attend. The Chinese performers were our favorite. Arlo Guthrie, a good customer, was always a pleasure to see when he came to town. Once listened to Carrie Fisher give a dialogue. How interesting listening to her talk about being married to Paul Simon and her role in "Star Wars." Oft times when the Lensic Board would hold one of their meetings, I would provide the coffee.

At this point in time, I was having so much fun at work that I pretty much stopped going out altogether. There were some exceptions: I would buy a growler, a friend would buy sushi and we would sit outside in the Railyard district underneath the water tower, discreetly drinking our beer. I did manage to go to a party. Didn't really know anybody. Had to take the bus to get there and when it came time to leave, had to get a ride home which was boring. In fact, the party was boring. Other than that, it was just, after making a deposit, going home after work. The fun I was having at work resulted in lots of customers wanting a selfie and a hug with me. I was happy to oblige. And yes, sometimes they wanted a kiss. One of my last customers was a young woman who wanted to hug me after I made her drink. She pressed her breasts against my chest.

EPILOGUE

Even though I cut my hours down from six days a week, 55 hours to four days a week, 24 hours, I was tired. At the end of the day, as mentioned, I would just collapse on the floor before getting up and doing my dishes in the back. I had played out my hand and it was time to throw in the cards. It was time to quit. It was time to sell the shop. But who would buy a shop that was slated to be demolished in about a year to make way for a hotel? Lucky for me, the owner of Henry and the Fish, excellent friend, said he would buy the shop and move everything into his cafe. So I sold the shop to Joe in January 2022 but nothing has happened to the shop since.

And for the woman with the bicycle? Well, the other day she came pounding on my door at home at eight o'clock at night, yelling at me and telling me I was a fake. Maybe I am. We are still friends tho and she has since moved to Port Townsend, Washington, just a few miles from Whidbey Island, where this story all began. It's good to still be friends with her.

Not long after selling the shop, I got drunk and my next door neighbor called an ambulance on me. We don't talk any more. Being retired now, I keep busy around the property and the house fixing things. Always something that needs to be fixed. Hopefully I still have a marriage after Helen reads this book.

Being a Christian, I'm happy to tell you to believe in Jesus for the saving of your soul. He's the reason I was the best barista. I had run the race and gone the distance. So after thirty years and a million customers, all I can say is "What a long strange trip it's been."

This book was finished on December 31, 2022.

Printed in the USA
CPSIA information can be obtained
at www.ICGtesting.com
LVHW030851290224
773137LV00008B/844